AF575180

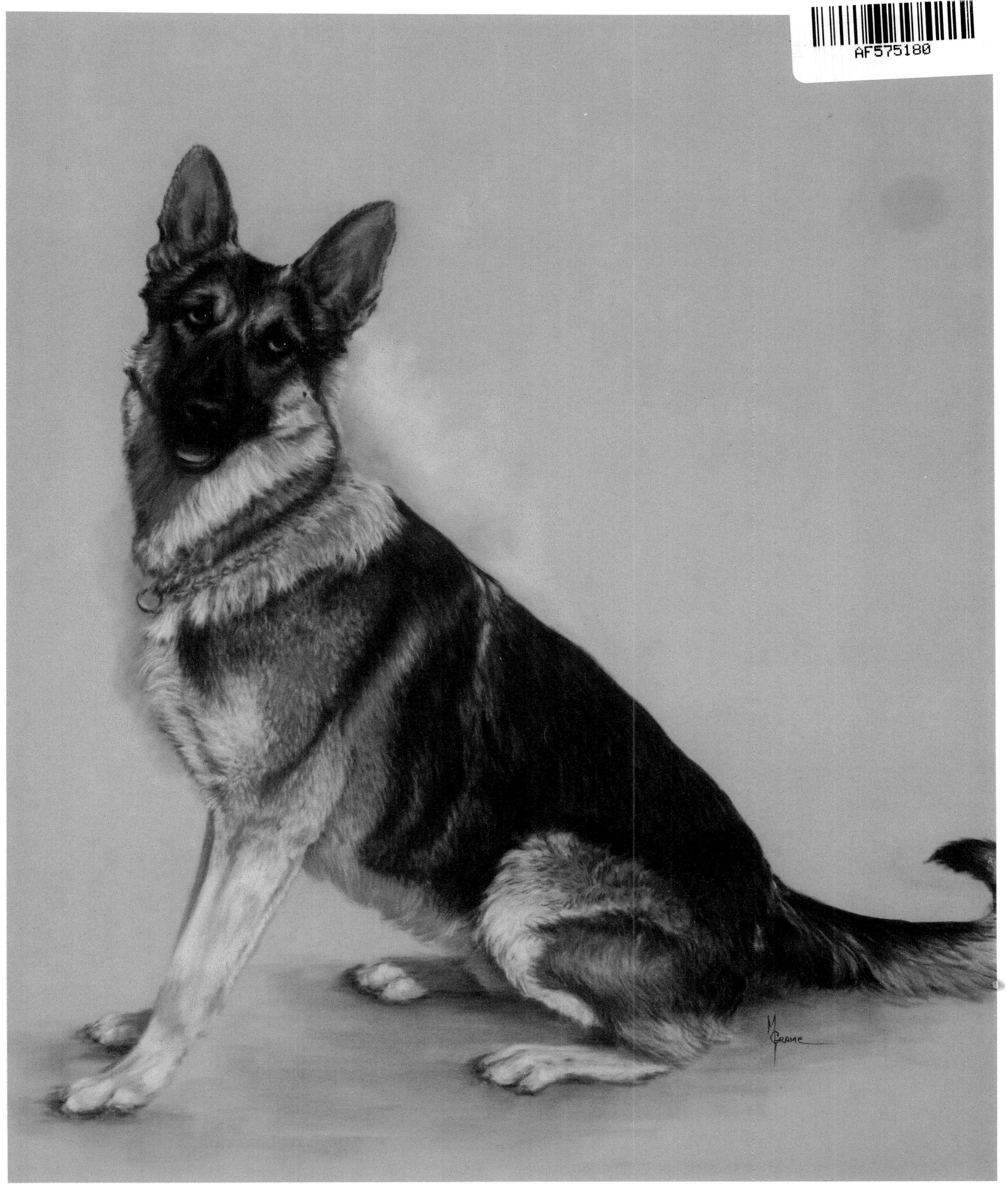

This painting of "Wolf" was done on tan velour paper. There is an abundance of detail here, accomplished with various long and short stroking. The hairs that turn toward the viewer are dots of color and value.

Introduction

Pastels have been in use since primitive man first "painted" on the walls of his cave with red, white and black "chalk." Many people think of pastel as a pale, insipid medium but in reality it can be anything—from delicate to dynamic!

If you have seen some of the beautiful paintings in museums rendered by impressionists such as Degas, you may have wondered about the permanency of the medium. But viewing those lovely examples will give you heart. The pastel pigment is extremely durable, and the painting surface will endure as well it if is 100% rag.

Working a finished picture with pastels is termed "painting" rather than drawing, although you can draw with the medium if you are so inclined.

Pastels are different from other media. Instead of premixing the colors to your specifications as with oil paints, you must "mix" or blend them on the painting surface itself. Many times you will find yourself hunting for a hue or a value that is not available in pastel. You will just have to experiment and work with what is available.

I hope you will enjoy painting animals in pastel and that this book will help you to hone your natural talent.

My sincere thanks to all my friends and students who helped in so many ways.

Marilyn Grame

To my dear husband, Bill —for his continuing support and his patience with my artistic temperament, my thanks always.

Materials

Soft pastels (or chalk pastels as they are sometimes called) are the purest form of pigment. The pigment is held together with just enough binder to make it into a stick. Pastels range from very soft, through several shapes and grades, to the hard pastel, and pastels in pencil form. Some of the less expensive pastels have too much filler added which weakens the pigment to the point that no matter how much you apply, you can't obtain the darks or the vibrancy of the finer grades—even the white is weak. So be sure to buy high quality materials, as it will make your job of painting much easier. Note—the pastels mentioned above are quite different from oil pastels, which will not be used in this book.

I own a great variety of brands and grades of soft, medium, and hard pastels. To really get in and work with them, I break them in halves or thirds and discard the paper wrappers. I lose track of the exact names and numbers of the colors and use them according to the character of the hue. My long experience with color in many media allows me to identify most of the colors, but it is not really necessary. It might be a good idea to make a color chart so you can replace the colors as you run out of them.

A brand new set of pastels looks so pretty all lined up and whole that some of my students find it difficult to break them, and they are inclined to return them carefully to their original box. I recommend separating them into groups of warm and cool for each color, then when you have a specific color in mind you can readily see the selection for that color. You can keep them in any container that works well for you—I keep mine in a cabinet with shallow removable drawers which I can spread out on my taboret for good visibility.

Before I start a painting, I select all the colors I think I will need and then keep them together until the picture is completed. Don't try to be neat and put them all back at the end of a session; you may not find the same colors again and, perhaps, you will not be able to match a previously used color. Don't put them away until you are completely finished with a painting.

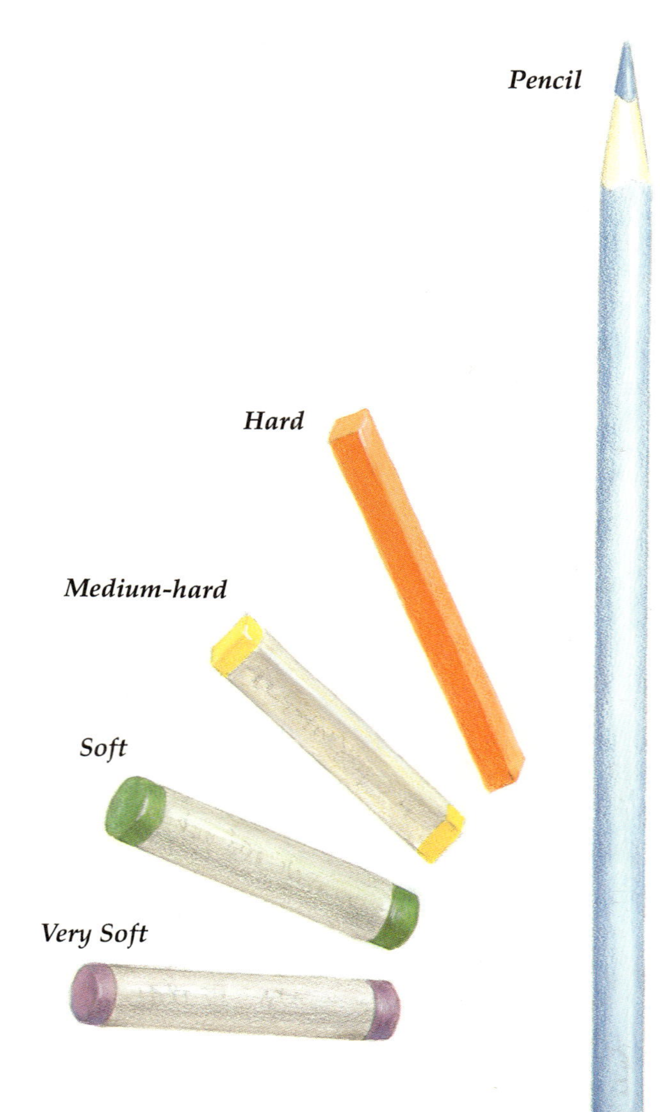

Other Materials

Smooth Board (to tape your paper to)
Masking Tape

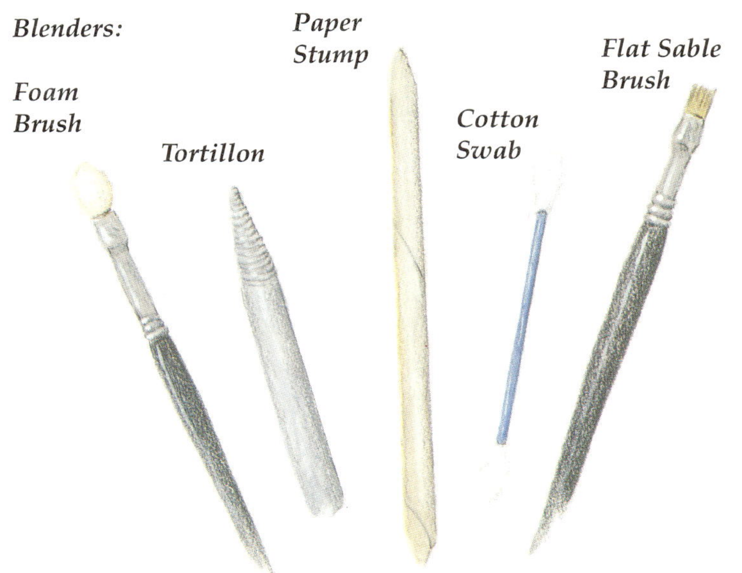

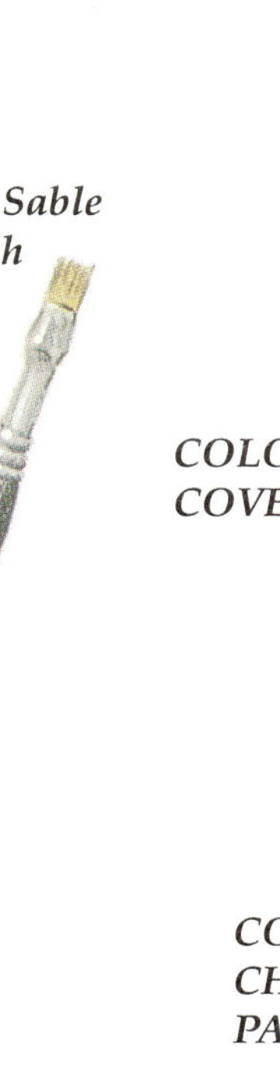

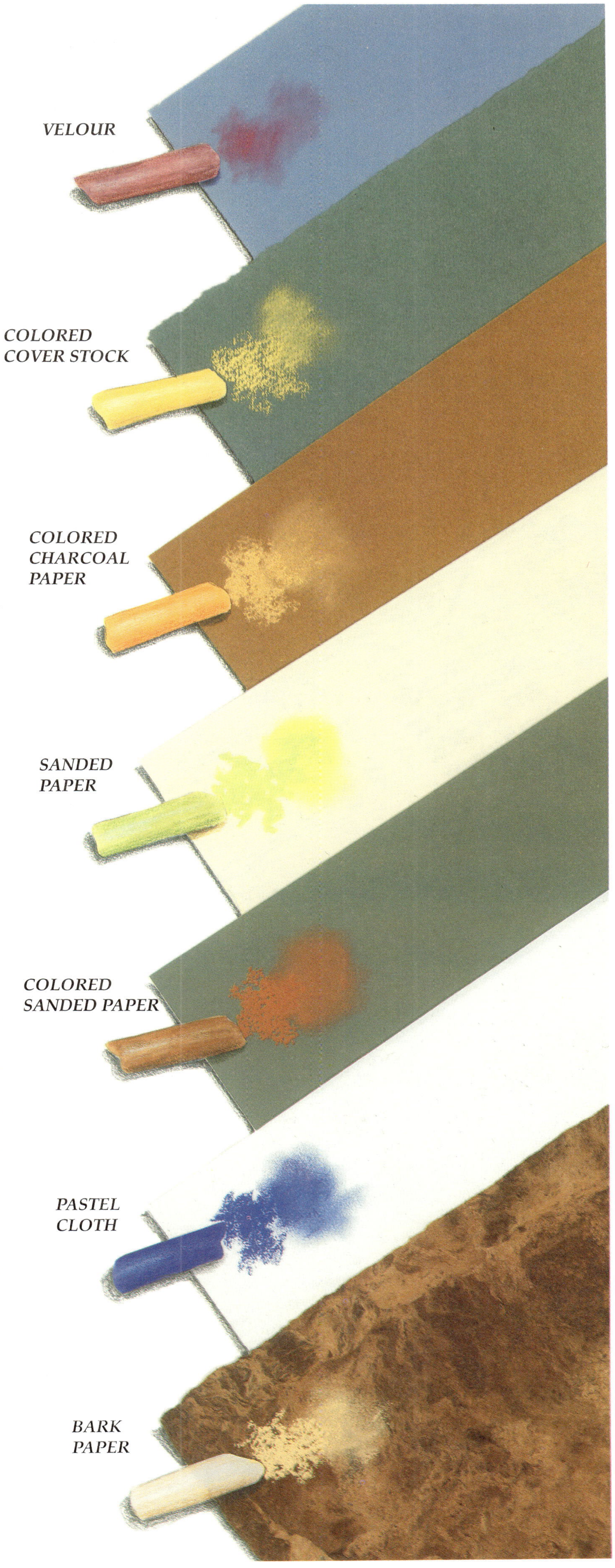

VELOUR

COLORED COVER STOCK

COLORED CHARCOAL PAPER

SANDED PAPER

COLORED SANDED PAPER

PASTEL CLOTH

BARK PAPER

Painting Surfaces And Techniques

There are many types and colors of surfaces on which to do a pastel painting: velour, colored cover stock, colored charcoal paper, sanded paper, pastel cloth, bark paper; in fact, any surface that has enough "tooth" (or surface texture) to hold the pigment. I will touch on some of these as we go along. (Certain grades of illustration board and watercolor paper can also be used.)

You can blend on some paper surfaces with your finger, a paper stump, a foam blender, or even with water, which reduces the pigment to a fluid.

My usual method is to use medium-soft pastels for the first application of pigment, hard for fine details, and soft (better pigment) for the final application. Medium-soft sticks also make very good "blenders."

Pressure is a very important factor in pastel painting. Sometimes the pressure is just "an angel's breath"; other times it is a bold application.

Stroking in different directions, either back and forth or in a circular motion, can help fill the surface and make it look smooth. As a first application it is best not to use too much pigment. On most papers this is the time to do your blending. After this, I recommend blending only with the pastels themselves. Next, "direct paint" with the side and/or the chiseled end of the pastel. Fine detail can be done with a pointed end (shaped with a razor blade or fine sandpaper), however, this "uses up" a lot of the pastel stick. Sometimes you can save the powder and use it with water and a brush for fine details (see page 18).

The examples on the right show the textures of the various painting surfaces used in this book.

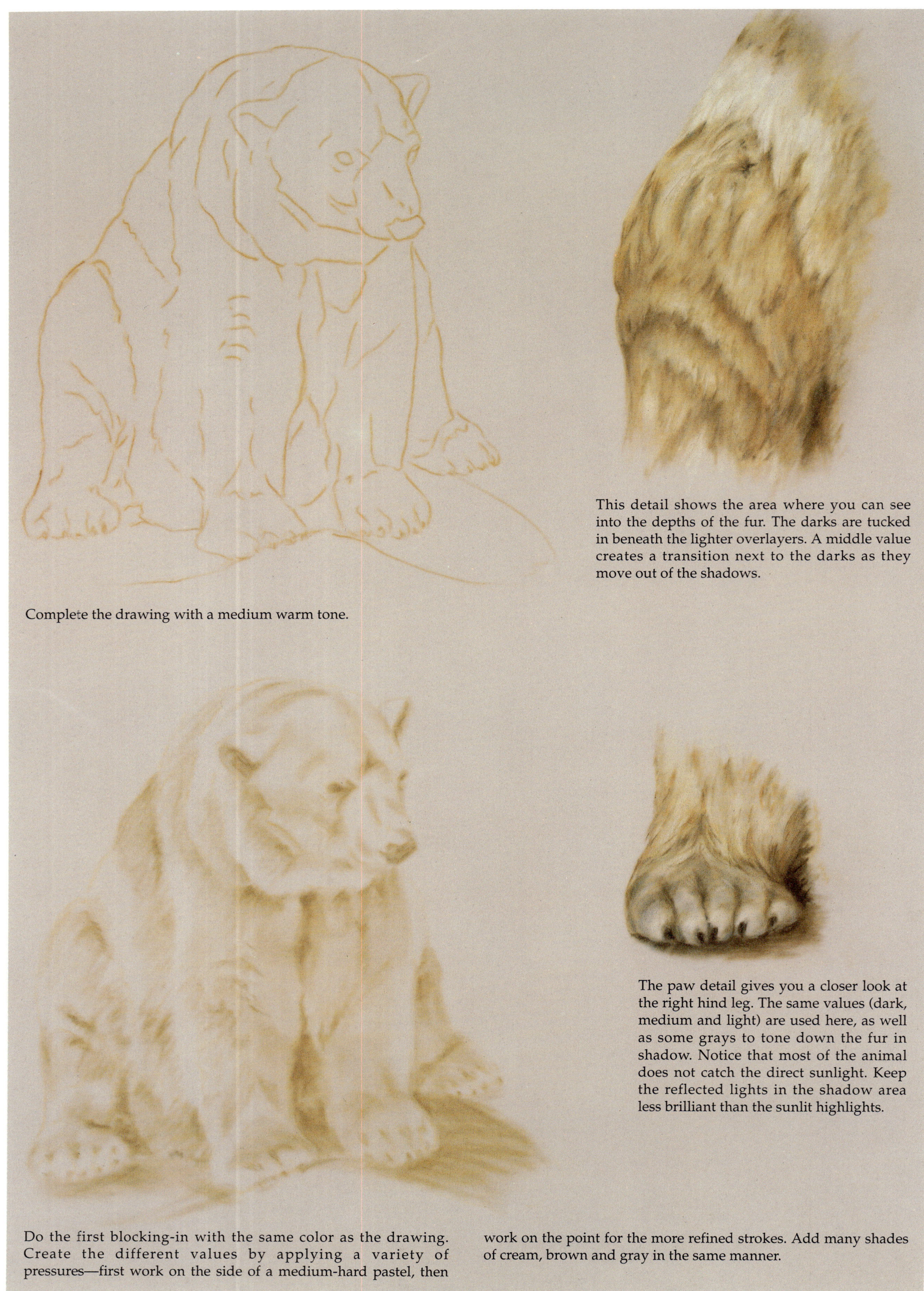

This detail shows the area where you can see into the depths of the fur. The darks are tucked in beneath the lighter overlayers. A middle value creates a transition next to the darks as they move out of the shadows.

Complete the drawing with a medium warm tone.

The paw detail gives you a closer look at the right hind leg. The same values (dark, medium and light) are used here, as well as some grays to tone down the fur in shadow. Notice that most of the animal does not catch the direct sunlight. Keep the reflected lights in the shadow area less brilliant than the sunlit highlights.

Do the first blocking-in with the same color as the drawing. Create the different values by applying a variety of pressures—first work on the side of a medium-hard pastel, then work on the point for the more refined strokes. Add many shades of cream, brown and gray in the same manner.

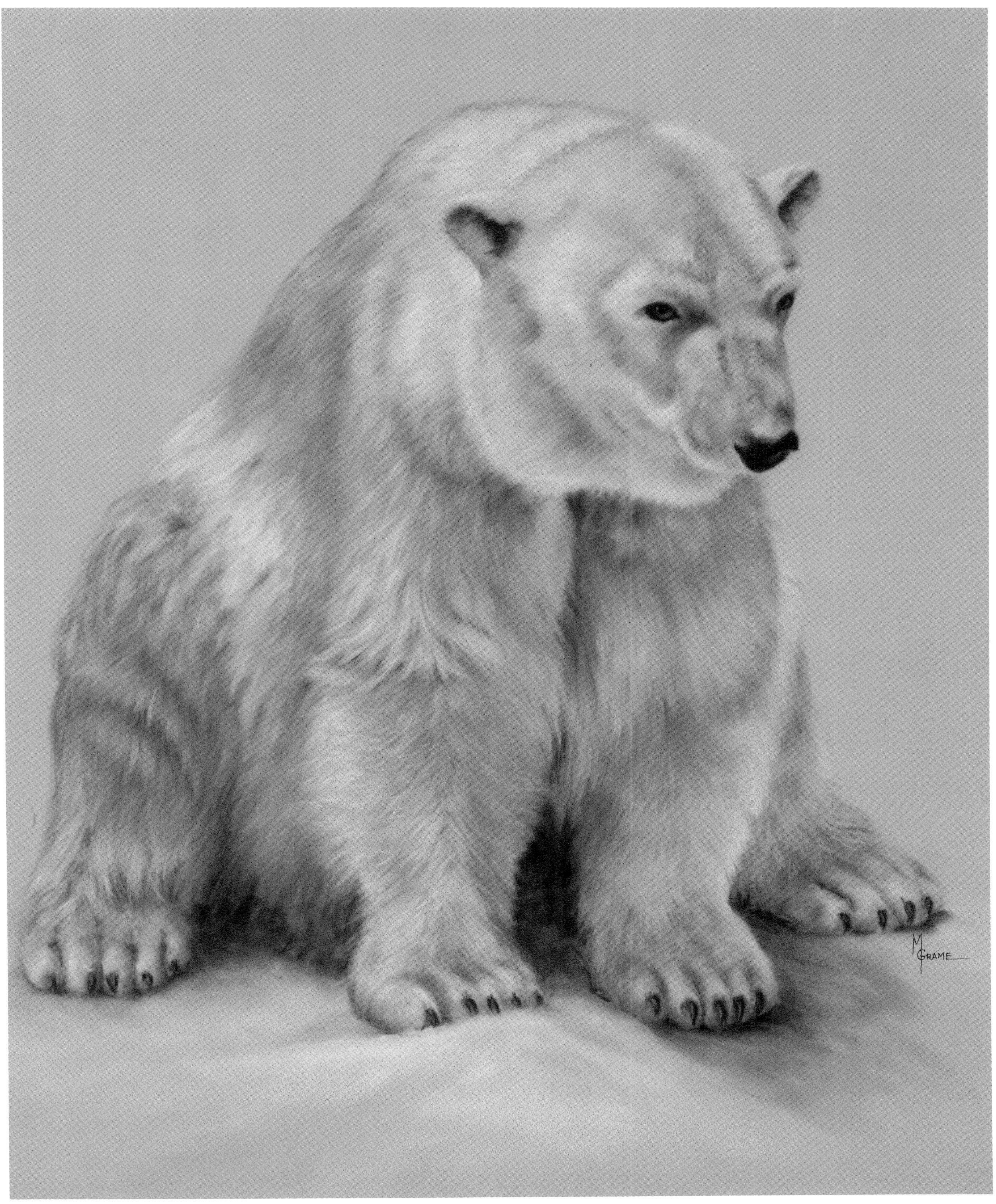

Gray velour was chosen for the cool environment of this polar bear. His warm colors contrast nicely with this background. You can see a difference, however, between these two pages because velour has a tendency to fade or change color. But if the entire surface is covered with pastel, this is less of a problem.

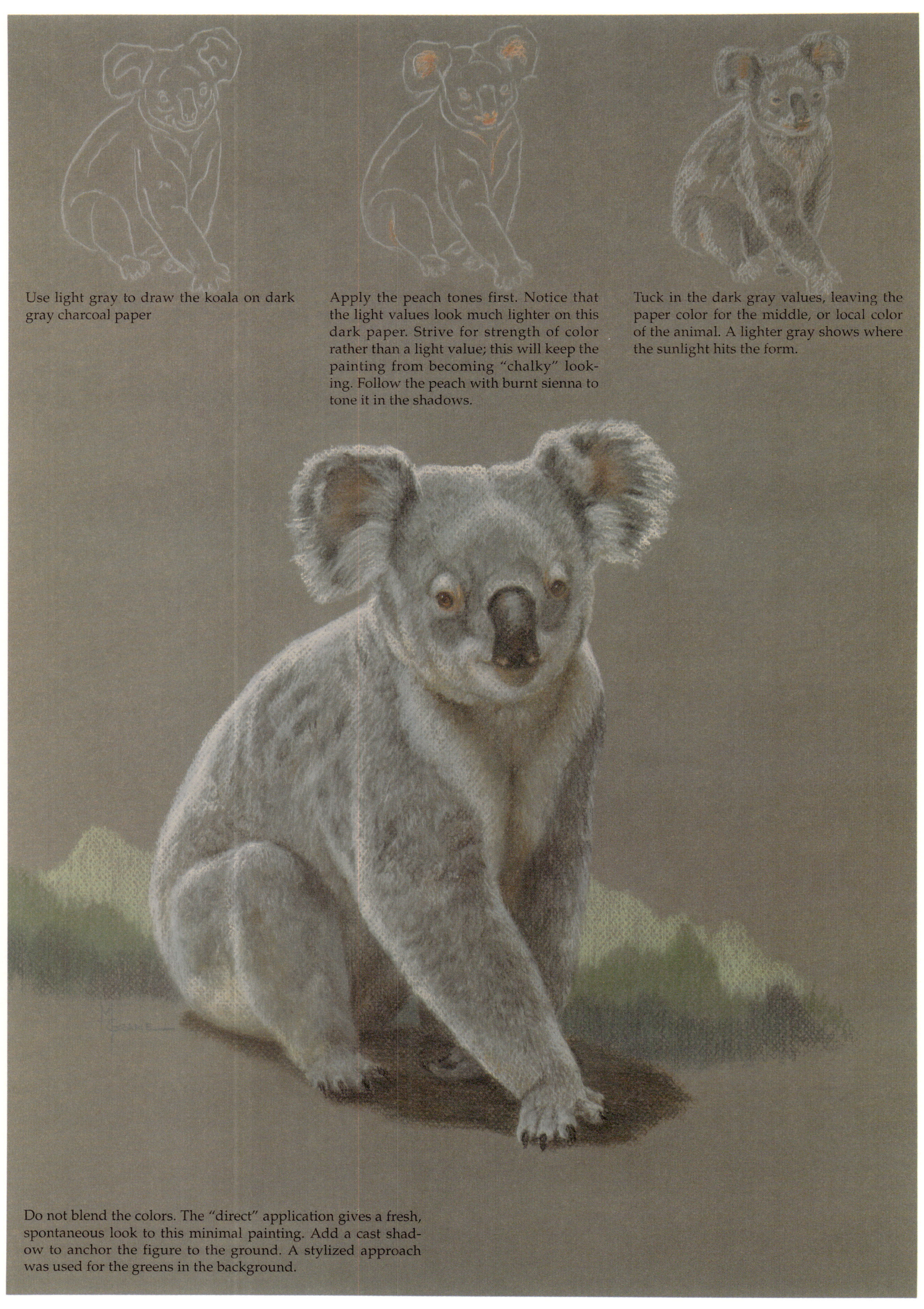

Use light gray to draw the koala on dark gray charcoal paper

Apply the peach tones first. Notice that the light values look much lighter on this dark paper. Strive for strength of color rather than a light value; this will keep the painting from becoming "chalky" looking. Follow the peach with burnt sienna to tone it in the shadows.

Tuck in the dark gray values, leaving the paper color for the middle, or local color of the animal. A lighter gray shows where the sunlight hits the form.

Do not blend the colors. The "direct" application gives a fresh, spontaneous look to this minimal painting. Add a cast shadow to anchor the figure to the ground. A stylized approach was used for the greens in the background.

When using a vivid paper like this it is best to experiment with the pastels on a scrap piece of the same paper. You will be surprised at the effect of the various colors against the yellow velour—they "read" differently from what you might expect. Bright colors can appear dull, or subtle colors so very dull as to be undesirable.

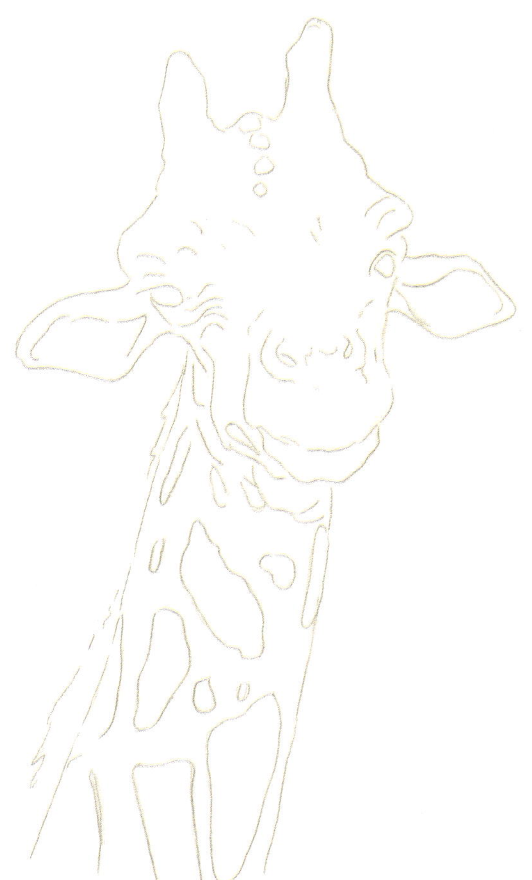

Cover the entire figure with various values of a raw sienna-type color, creating the contour of the animal. Work the spots in over this color. (The undercoat adds to the strength of the burnt sienna and darker umbers.)

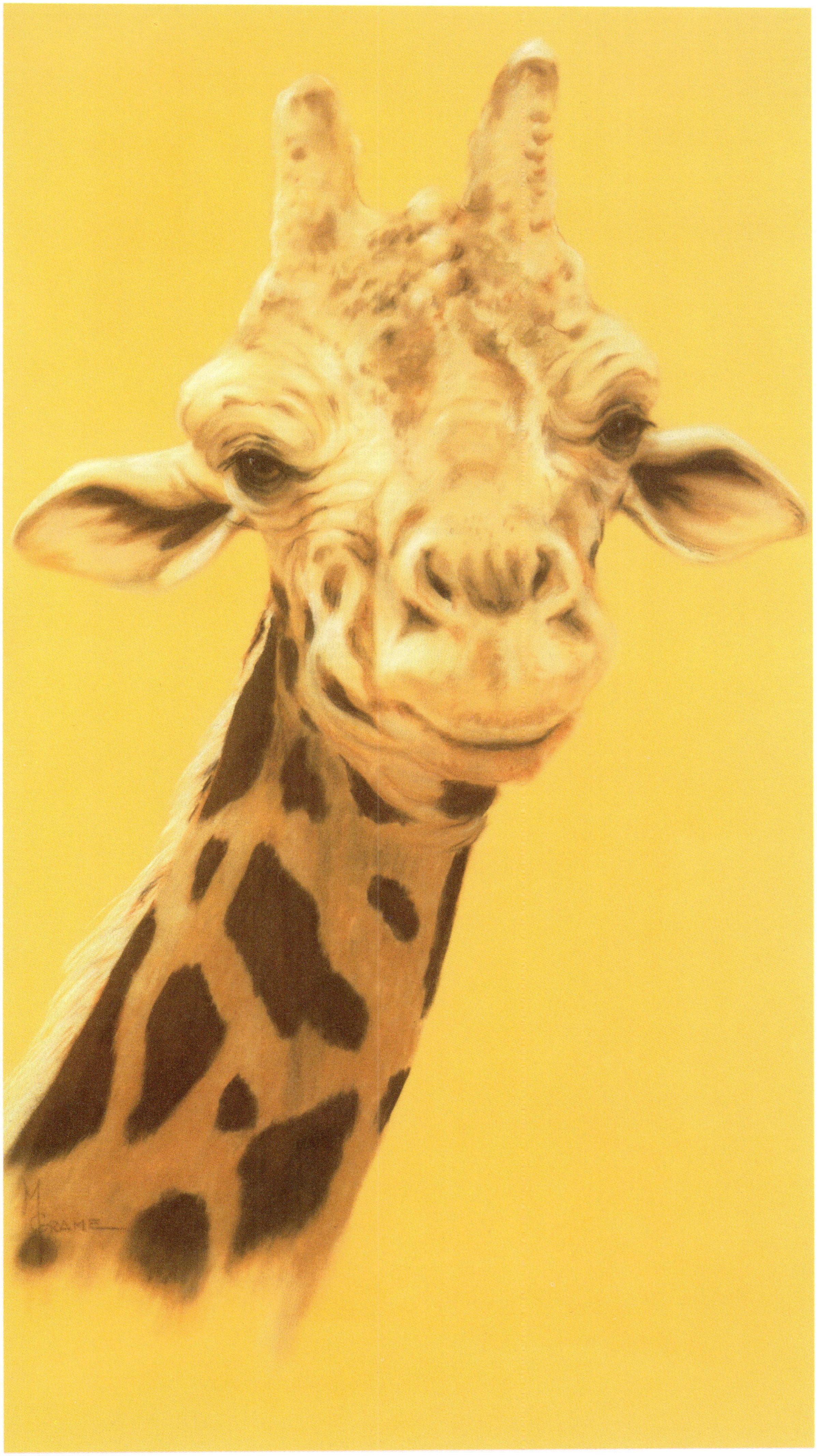

Use a combination of a dull middle value umber and warm oranges in the shadow areas. Light, creamy highlights lend the feeling of sunshine. The reflected light on the upper lip and various places throughout the light areas have a "transition" color in the yellow-orange family.

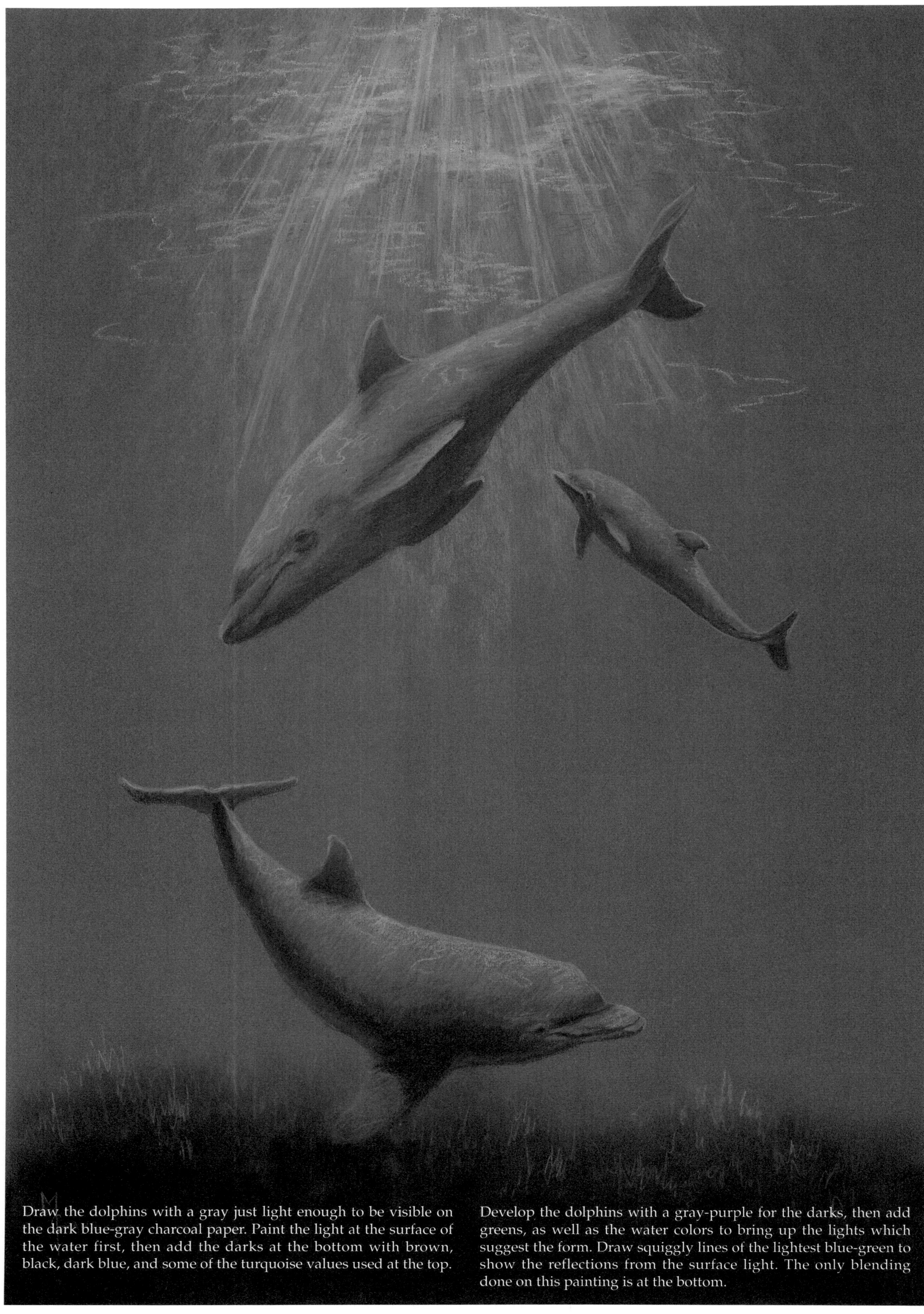

Draw the dolphins with a gray just light enough to be visible on the dark blue-gray charcoal paper. Paint the light at the surface of the water first, then add the darks at the bottom with brown, black, dark blue, and some of the turquoise values used at the top.

Develop the dolphins with a gray-purple for the darks, then add greens, as well as the water colors to bring up the lights which suggest the form. Draw squiggly lines of the lightest blue-green to show the reflections from the surface light. The only blending done on this painting is at the bottom.

To help keep track of the colors of this rooster, complete the drawing with the various hues. This was done on a fine sanded paper.

The first blocking-in made me feel like I was back in my childhood with my coloring book. Actually, that is what I was doing—filling in the blanks.

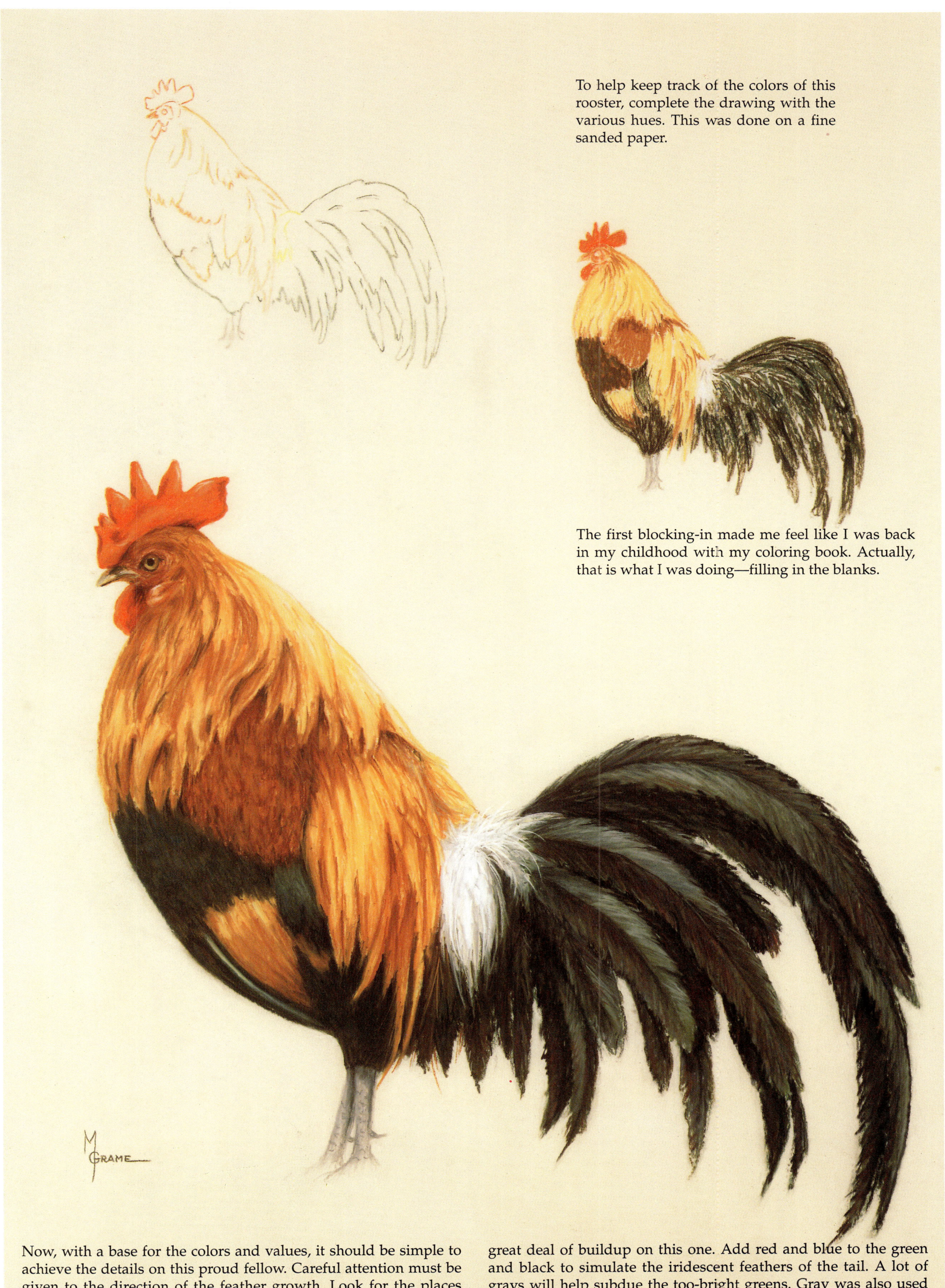

Now, with a base for the colors and values, it should be simple to achieve the details on this proud fellow. Careful attention must be given to the direction of the feather growth. Look for the places where feathers overlap and cast shadows on others. There is a great deal of buildup on this one. Add red and blue to the green and black to simulate the iridescent feathers of the tail. A lot of grays will help subdue the too-bright greens. Gray was also used for the cool highlights.

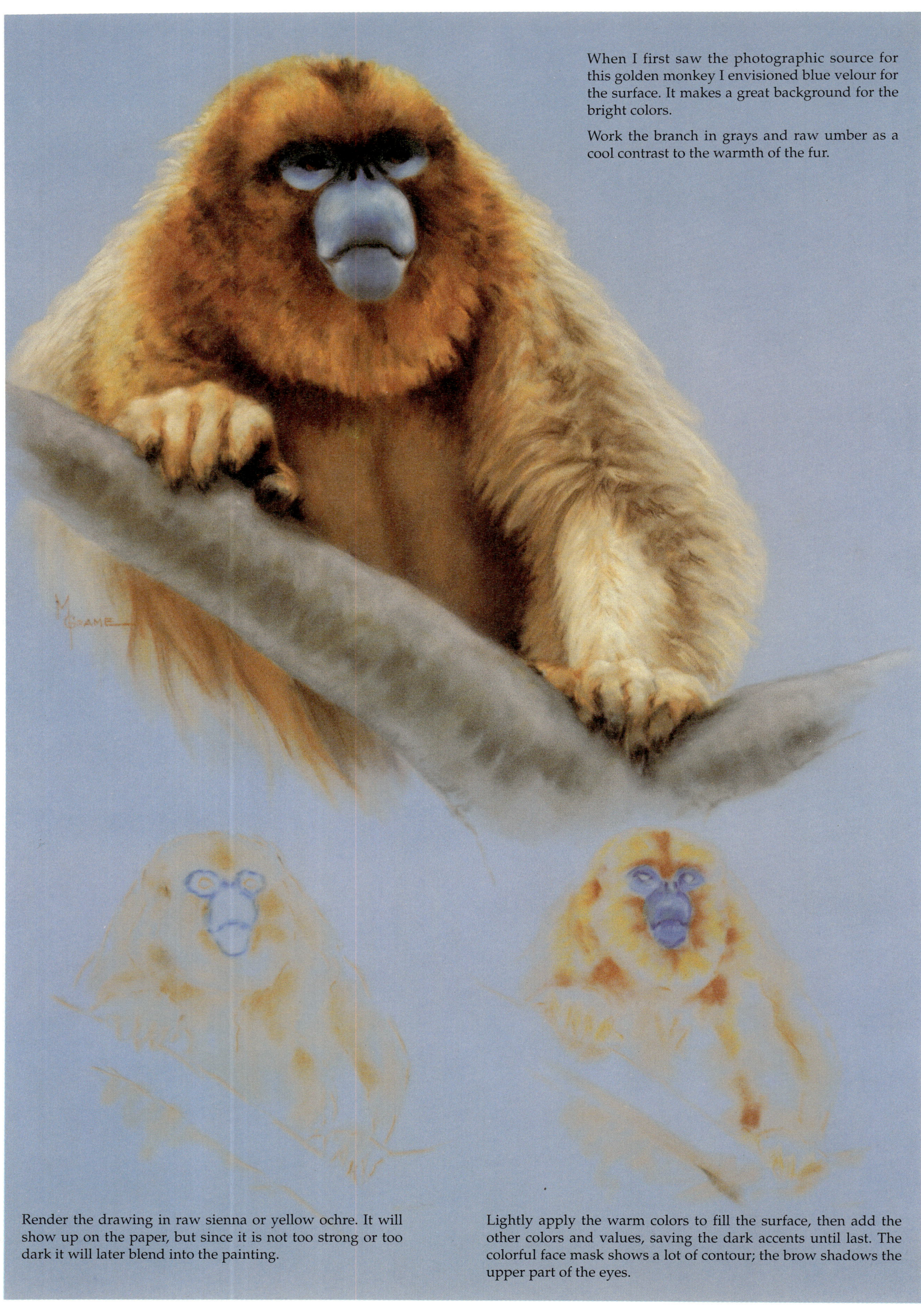

When I first saw the photographic source for this golden monkey I envisioned blue velour for the surface. It makes a great background for the bright colors.

Work the branch in grays and raw umber as a cool contrast to the warmth of the fur.

Render the drawing in raw sienna or yellow ochre. It will show up on the paper, but since it is not too strong or too dark it will later blend into the painting.

Lightly apply the warm colors to fill the surface, then add the other colors and values, saving the dark accents until last. The colorful face mask shows a lot of contour; the brow shadows the upper part of the eyes.

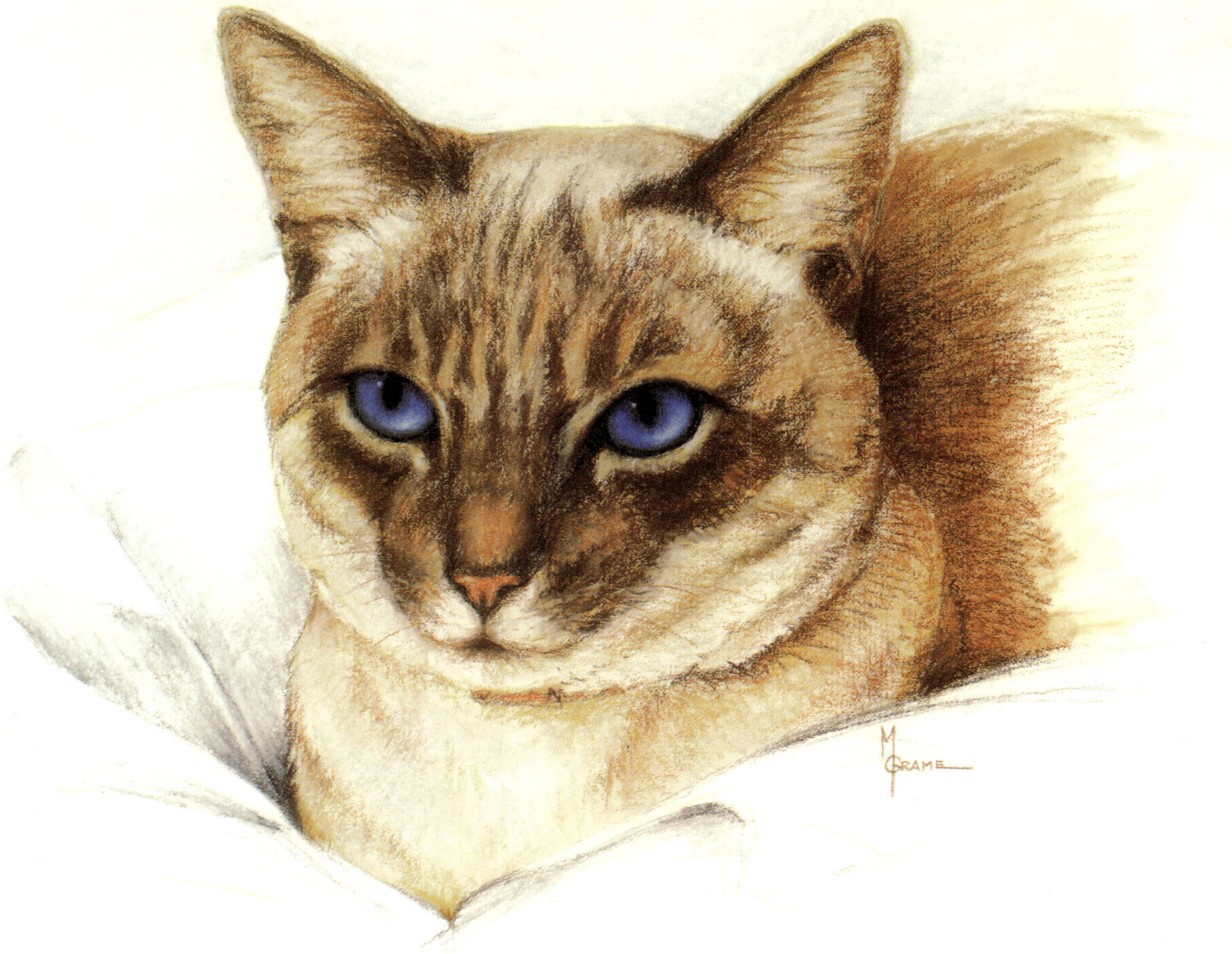

This lovely Siamese was done on a special pastel cloth. Since it is white, I created the "local color" with pastels and paint thinner. This saves most of the "tooth" of the paper for subsequent applications.

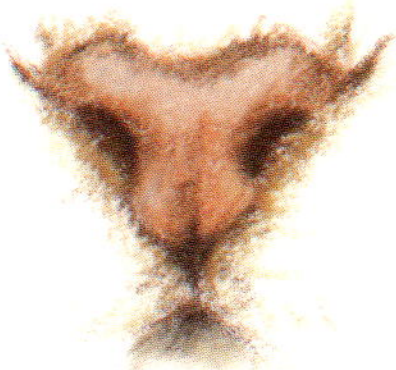

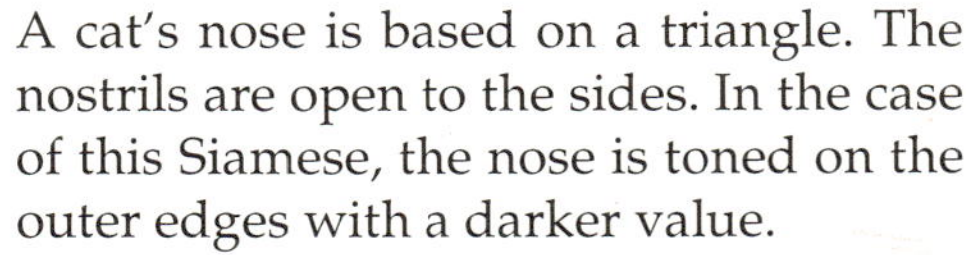

A cat's nose is based on a triangle. The nostrils are open to the sides. In the case of this Siamese, the nose is toned on the outer edges with a darker value.

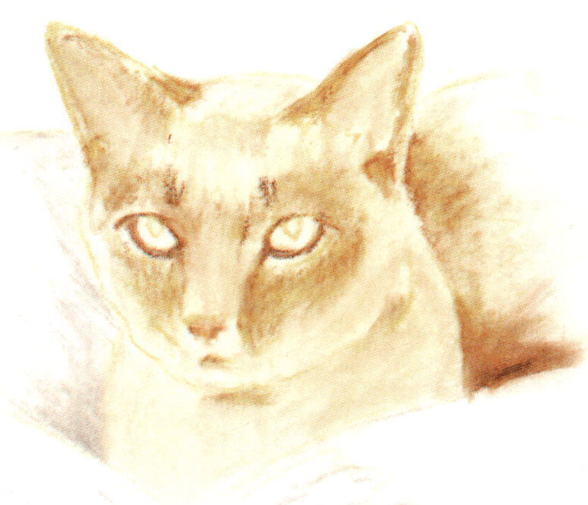

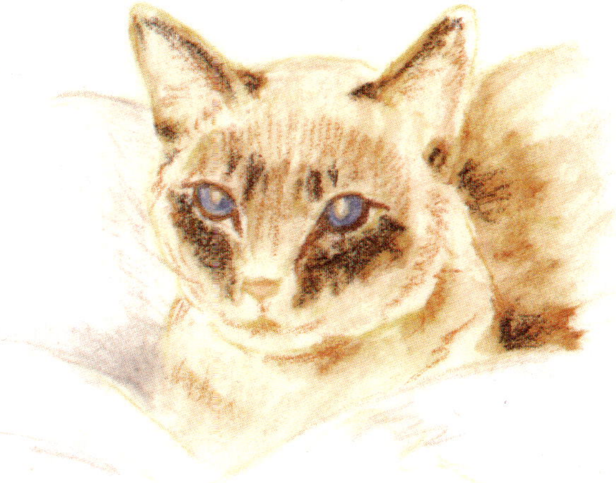

Complete the drawing with a tan pastel pencil, then fill in with pastels and brush with paint thinner. Accuracy is not a factor at this point, in fact, it may look fairly sloppy. You have probably discovered by now that pastels have a very ugly stage. But, just keep working and it will all come together! After the thinner is dry, begin to apply the darker values to the face with dry pastels. Then add the lighter hues. Some of the undercolor can become an integral part of the whole, and in some areas there is very minimal painting. The exotic eyes are a lovely cerulean blue with darker areas around the pupils. The glow opposite the highlight gives them life.

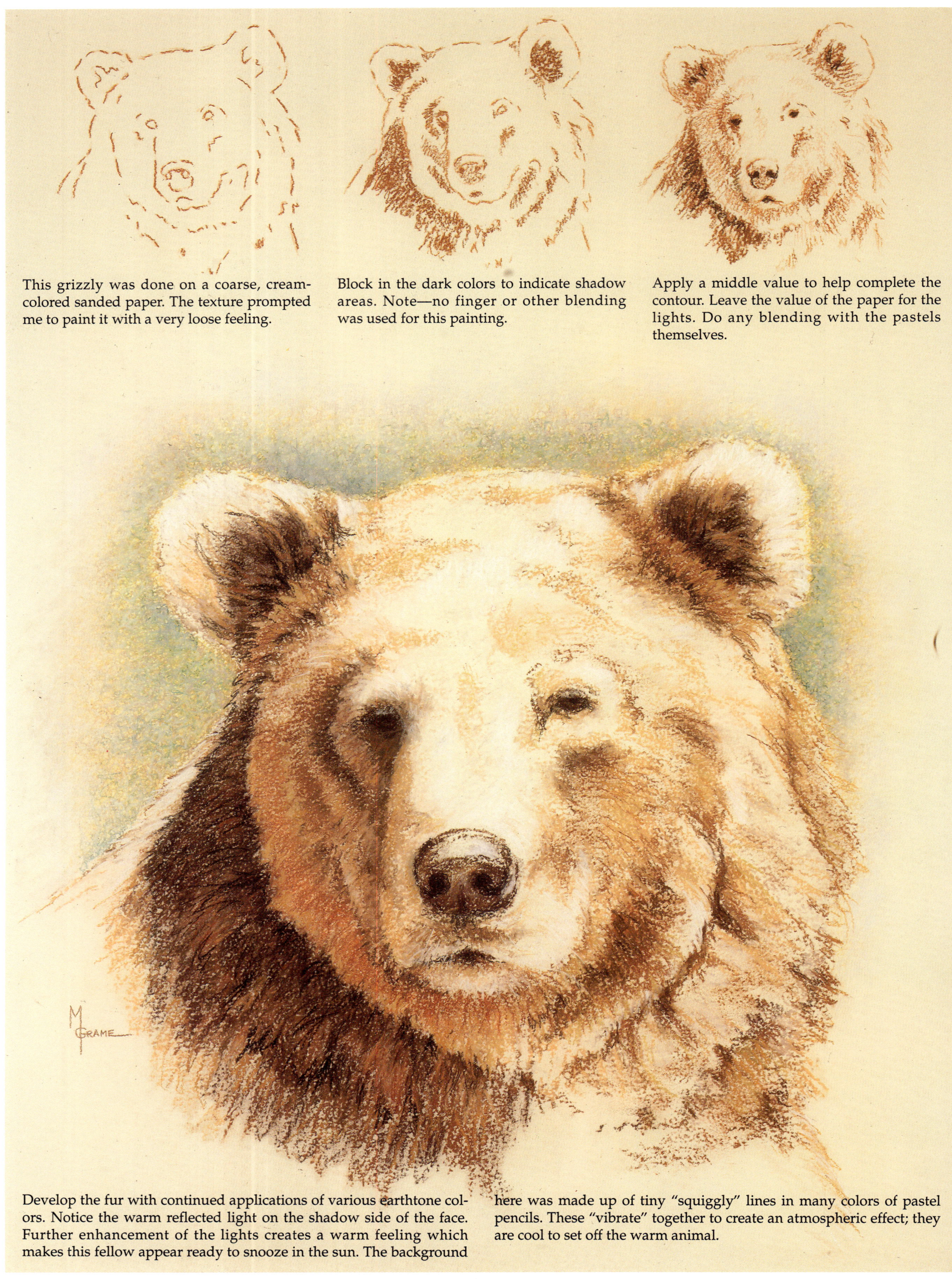

This grizzly was done on a coarse, cream-colored sanded paper. The texture prompted me to paint it with a very loose feeling.

Block in the dark colors to indicate shadow areas. Note—no finger or other blending was used for this painting.

Apply a middle value to help complete the contour. Leave the value of the paper for the lights. Do any blending with the pastels themselves.

Develop the fur with continued applications of various earthtone colors. Notice the warm reflected light on the shadow side of the face. Further enhancement of the lights creates a warm feeling which makes this fellow appear ready to snooze in the sun. The background here was made up of tiny "squiggly" lines in many colors of pastel pencils. These "vibrate" together to create an atmospheric effect; they are cool to set off the warm animal.

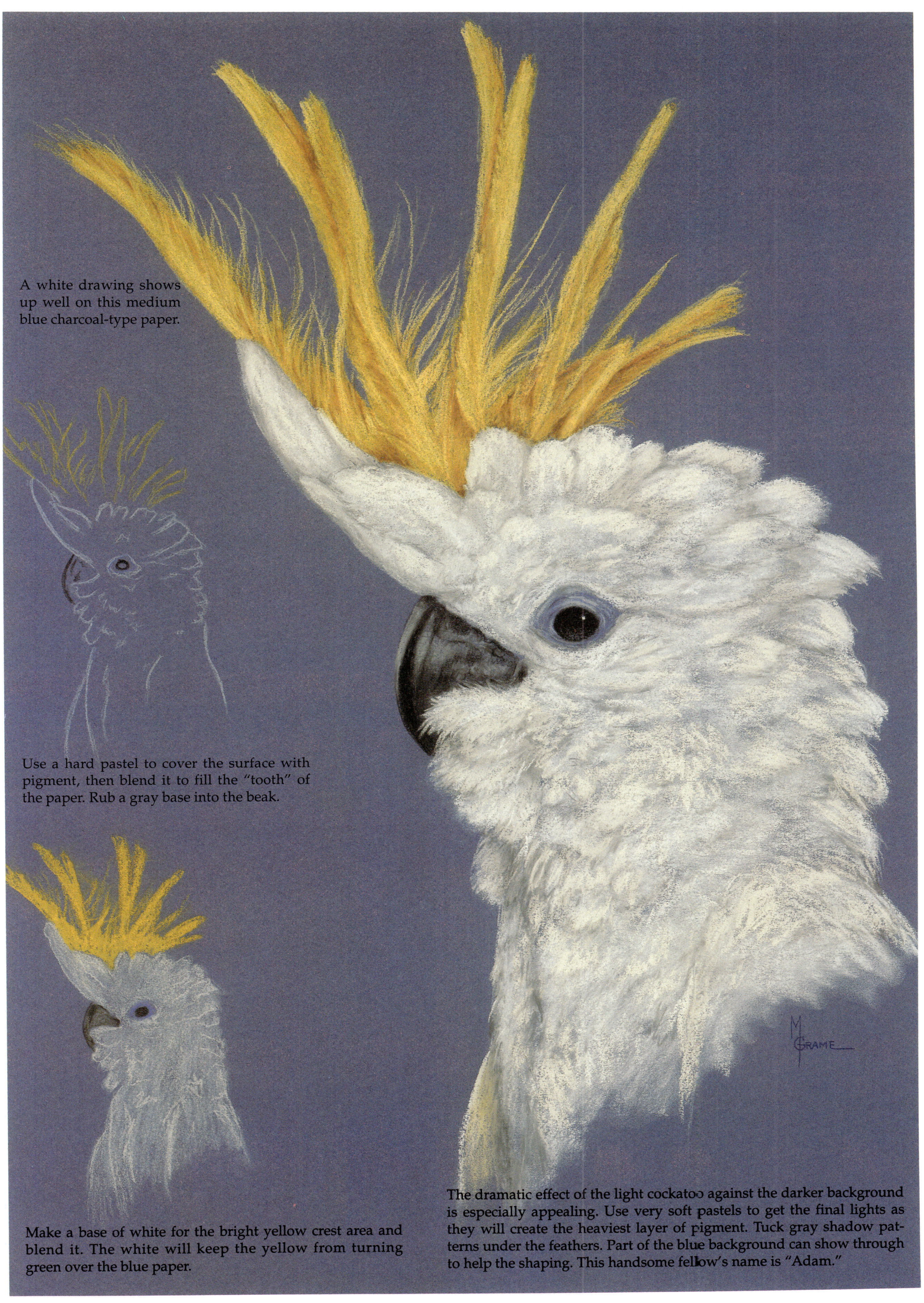

A white drawing shows up well on this medium blue charcoal-type paper.

Use a hard pastel to cover the surface with pigment, then blend it to fill the "tooth" of the paper. Rub a gray base into the beak.

Make a base of white for the bright yellow crest area and blend it. The white will keep the yellow from turning green over the blue paper.

The dramatic effect of the light cockatoo against the darker background is especially appealing. Use very soft pastels to get the final lights as they will create the heaviest layer of pigment. Tuck gray shadow patterns under the feathers. Part of the blue background can show through to help the shaping. This handsome fellow's name is "Adam."

This painting was done on bark paper. Bark paper has two distinct sides—one slick and smooth, the other quite rough. I chose to use the rough side to take advantage of the "tooth." The irregular texture of the paper is a bonus for depicting the rough-skinned elephant. Each piece of this handmade paper is unique, as is apparent when comparing these facing pages.

Transfer the drawing with a light gray pastel so it will be visible while blocking it in.

The first application will appear grainy as the high points of the paper pick up the pastel.

First block in the darks with a dark brown. This color was very close to the tone of the paper, yet still visible as a shadow design.

Start the light or sunshine areas with the lightest gray. As color is added over color they will mix, making a slightly smoother look. Apply lighter brown and darker gray; they make good blenders and help tone down some of the mid-value shadowed areas.

Add accents (blacks) and extra highlights (white). Then, most important to the impact of the picture, apply WARM REFLECTED LIGHTS to help separate the image from the background.

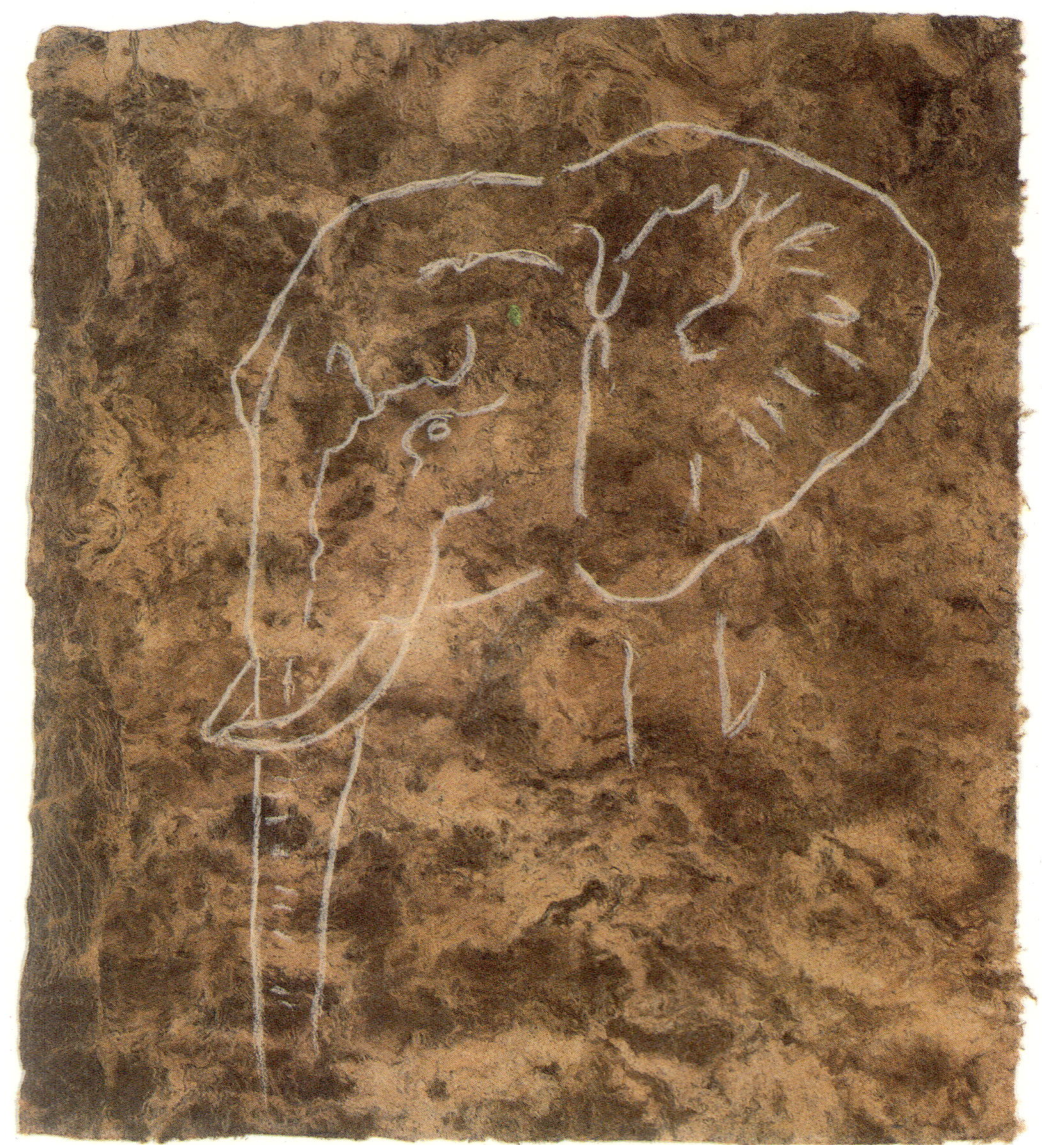

COLORS USED:

2 grays, black and white
2 browns
2 ochre/raw siennas

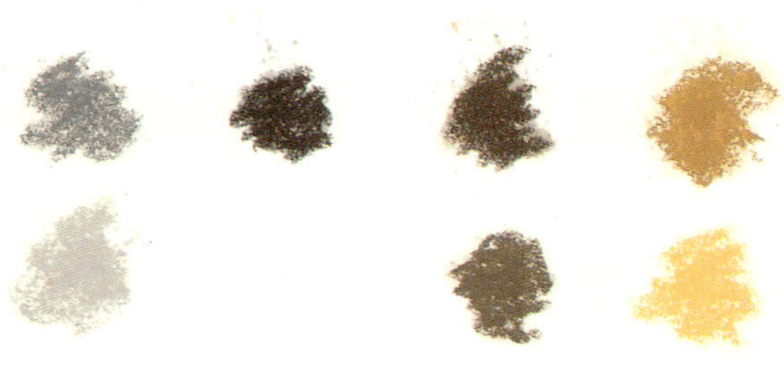

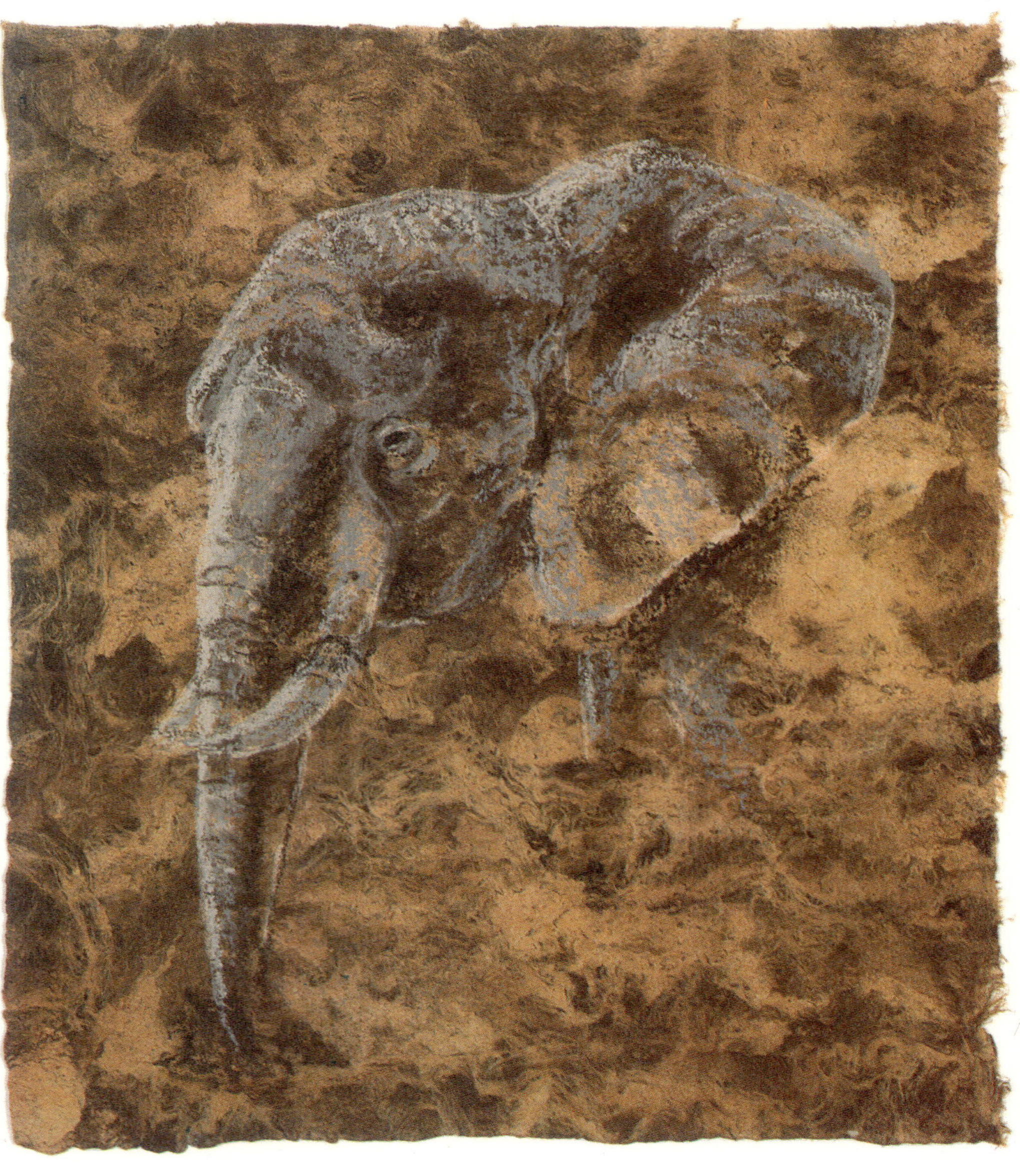

The bottom of the trunk fades out unevenly in a "painterly" manner.

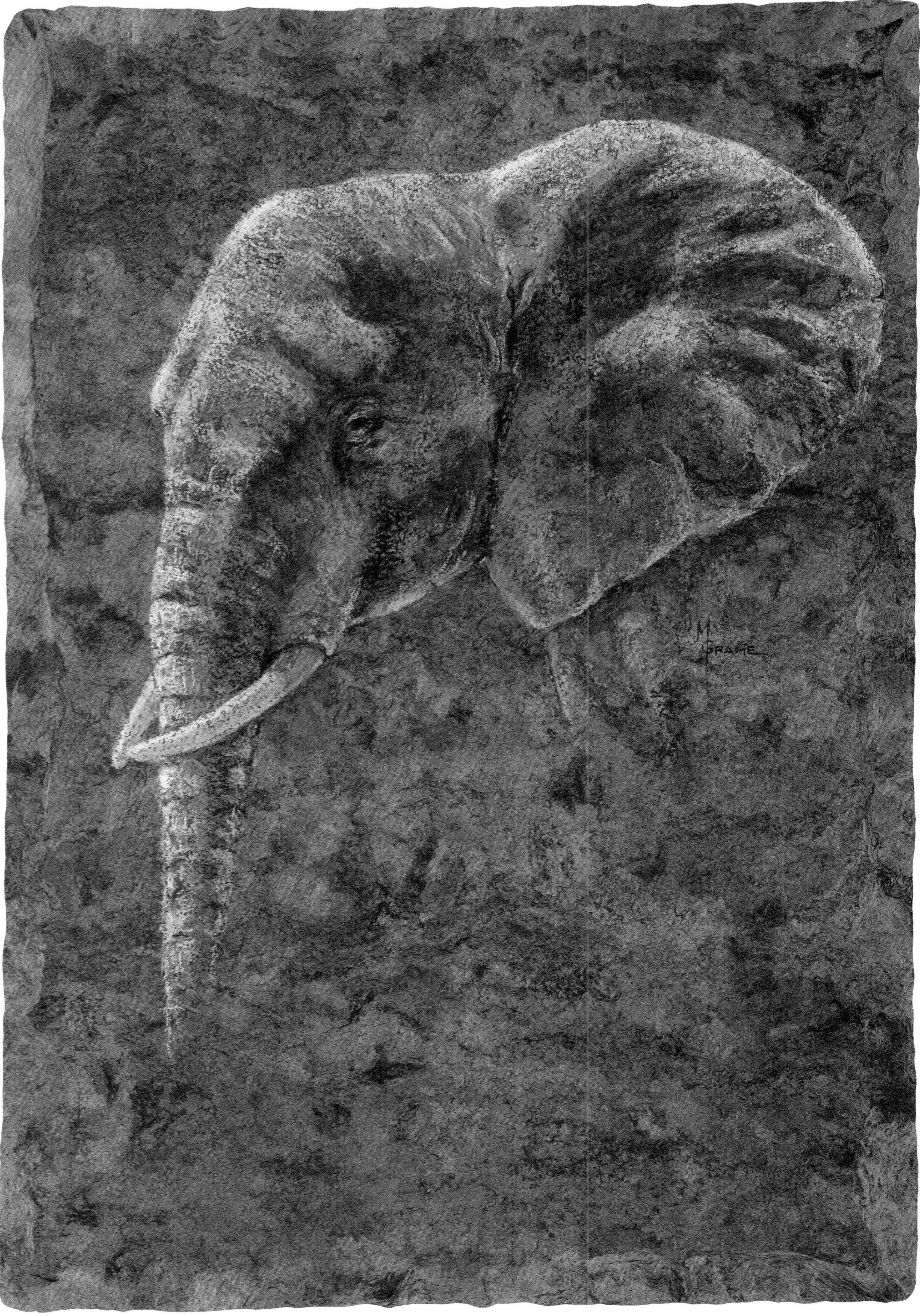

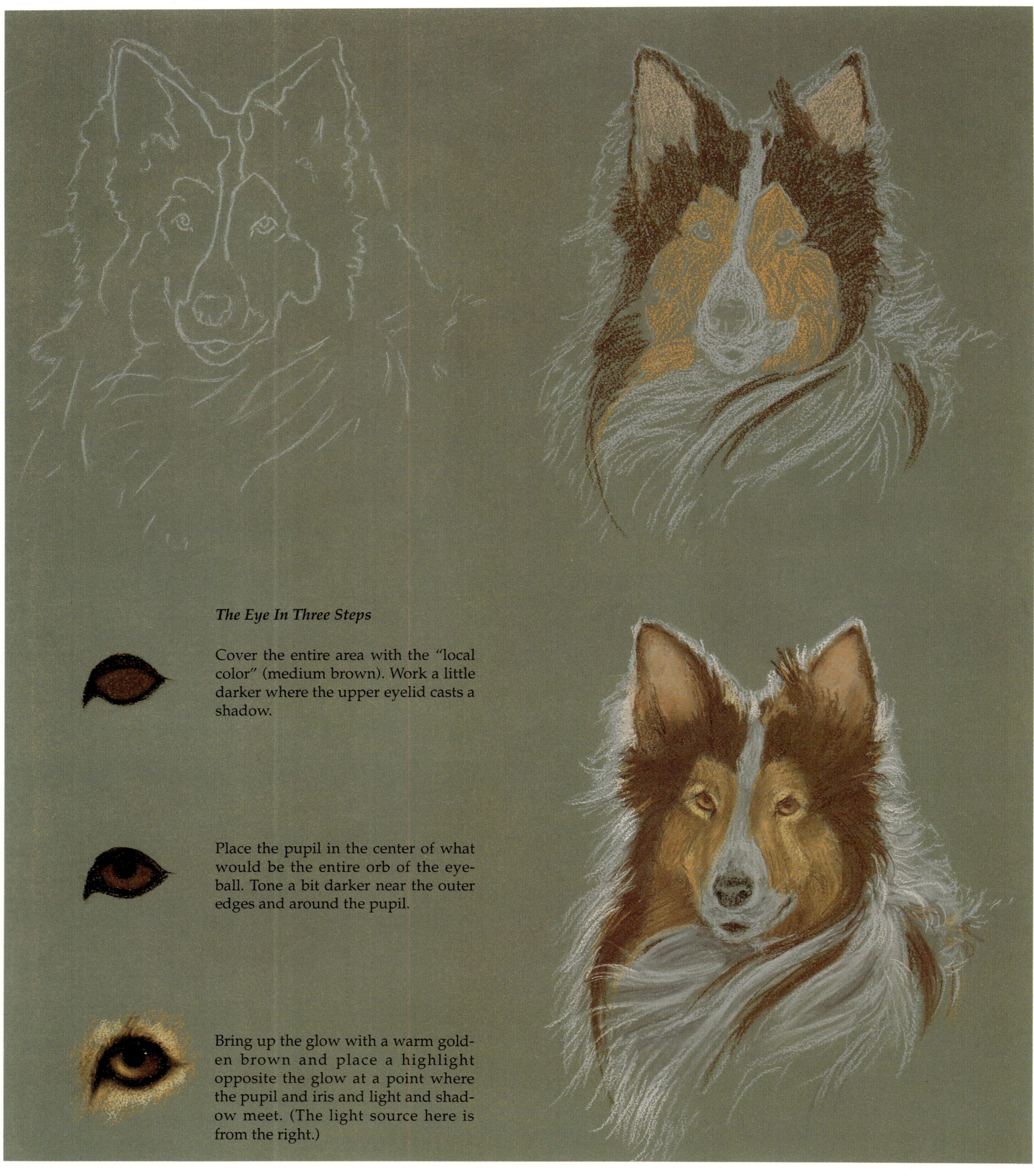

The Eye In Three Steps

Cover the entire area with the "local color" (medium brown). Work a little darker where the upper eyelid casts a shadow.

Place the pupil in the center of what would be the entire orb of the eyeball. Tone a bit darker near the outer edges and around the pupil.

Bring up the glow with a warm golden brown and place a highlight opposite the glow at a point where the pupil and iris and light and shadow meet. (The light source here is from the right.)

This painting was done on green fine sanded paper that has a slightly grainy "tooth." It is subtle enough to serve as a simple background for the colors of the dog, and it is enough of a medium value to further enhance the aura of backlighting that makes the picture so dynamic. The simple drawing is done in white with close attention to the features and their relationship to each other. The outside hair is done very sketchily with no real commitment at present.

Make the first application of color heavy enough so there is sufficient pigment to blend into the surface with your finger. This base-coat is necessary as you don't want too much of the green paper to show within the subject. The "ugly stage" of pastel painting is evident here.

After the base is laid in, work various colors into it, keeping all the shadow areas gray. The colors "vibrate" with each other to simulate the dog's true color which otherwise might not have been accomplished with the available selection. Add more darks in various earthtones and some reddish-brown. Don't let the lights on the face compete with the "aura," which is done with softer pastels to take advantage of the strength of the pigments.

This lovely sheltie is my friend, Doyle (registered name, "Capri's Gold Touch O' Windose").

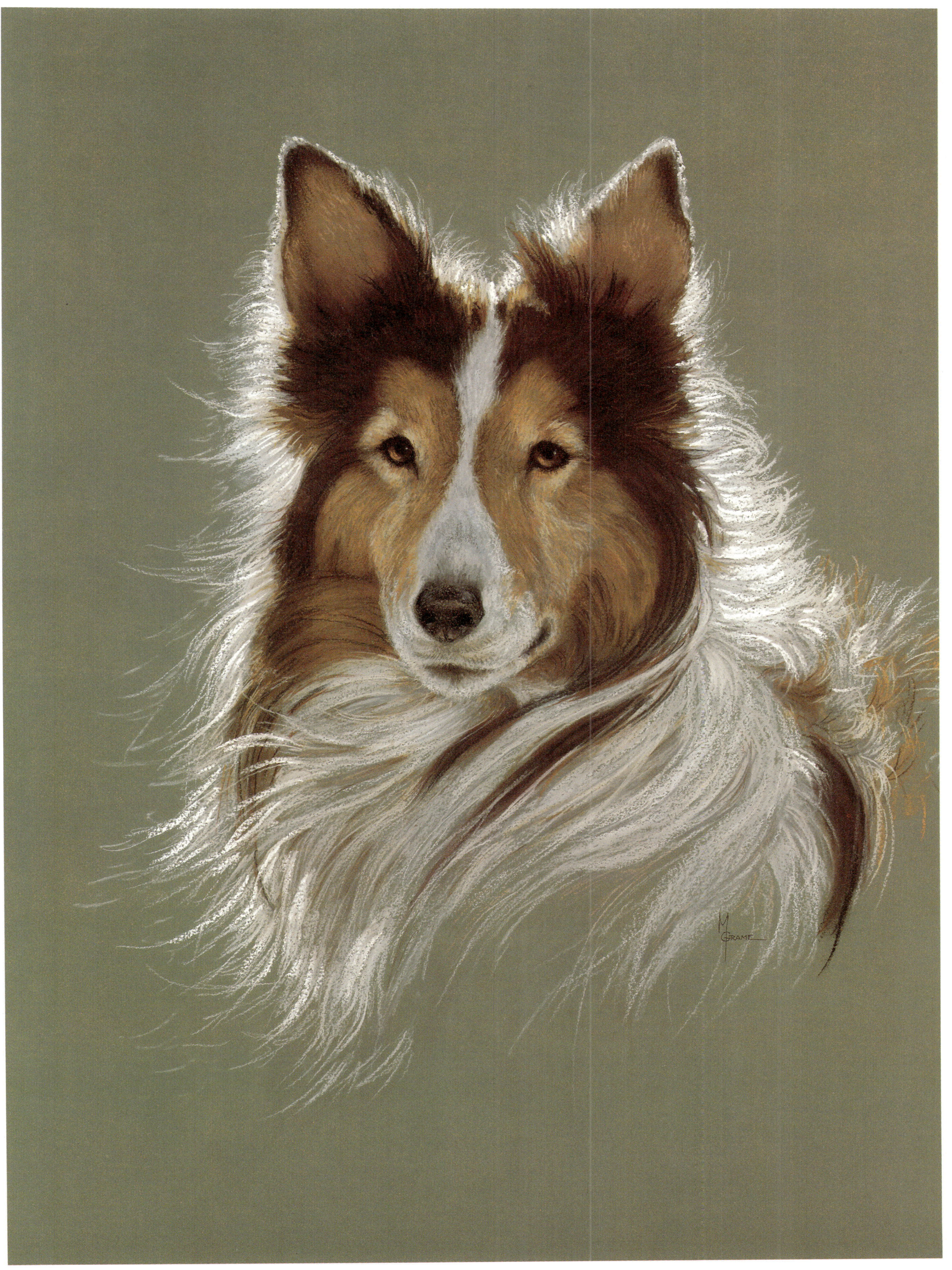
GRAME

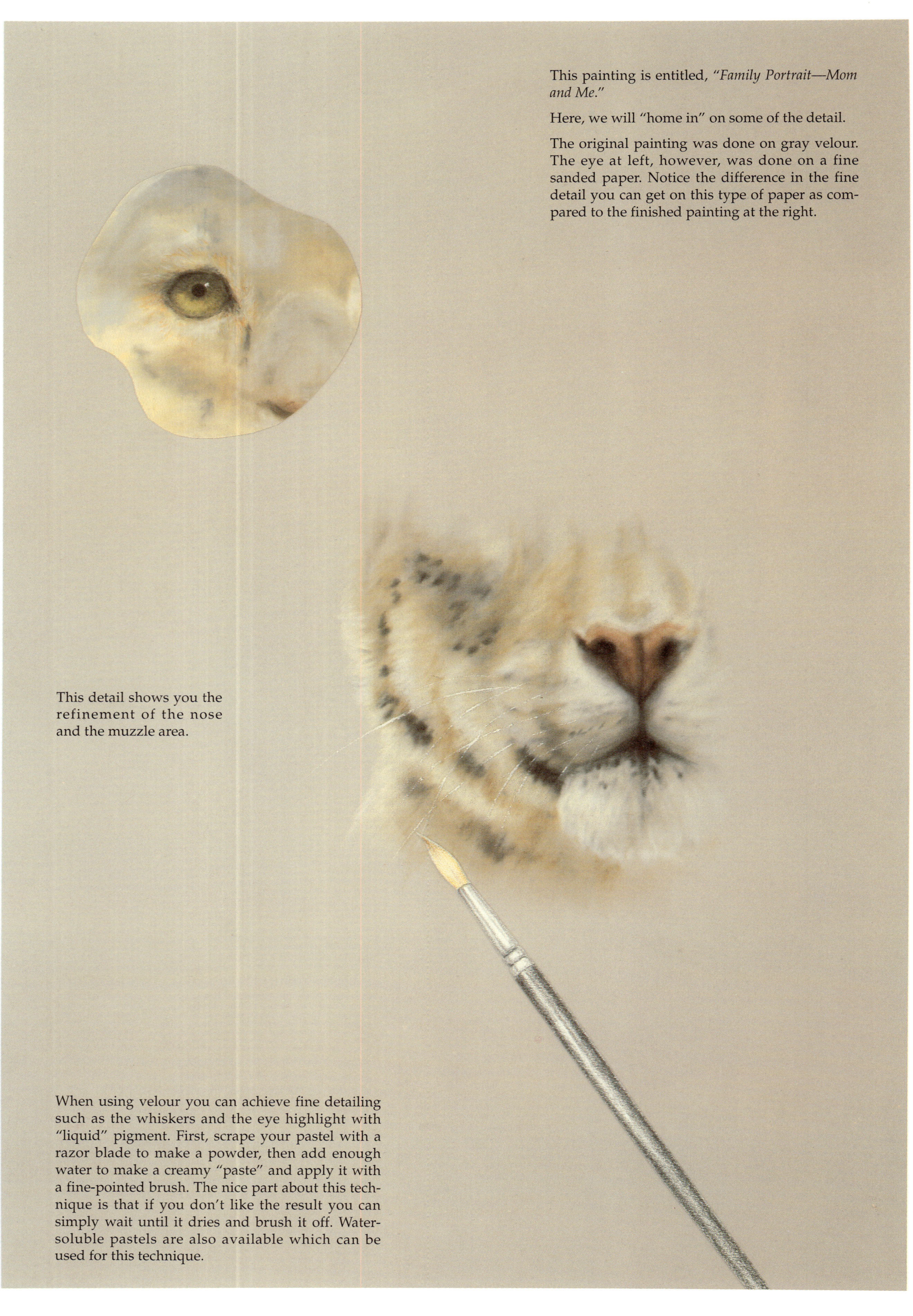

This painting is entitled, *"Family Portrait—Mom and Me."*

Here, we will "home in" on some of the detail.

The original painting was done on gray velour. The eye at left, however, was done on a fine sanded paper. Notice the difference in the fine detail you can get on this type of paper as compared to the finished painting at the right.

This detail shows you the refinement of the nose and the muzzle area.

When using velour you can achieve fine detailing such as the whiskers and the eye highlight with "liquid" pigment. First, scrape your pastel with a razor blade to make a powder, then add enough water to make a creamy "paste" and apply it with a fine-pointed brush. The nice part about this technique is that if you don't like the result you can simply wait until it dries and brush it off. Water-soluble pastels are also available which can be used for this technique.

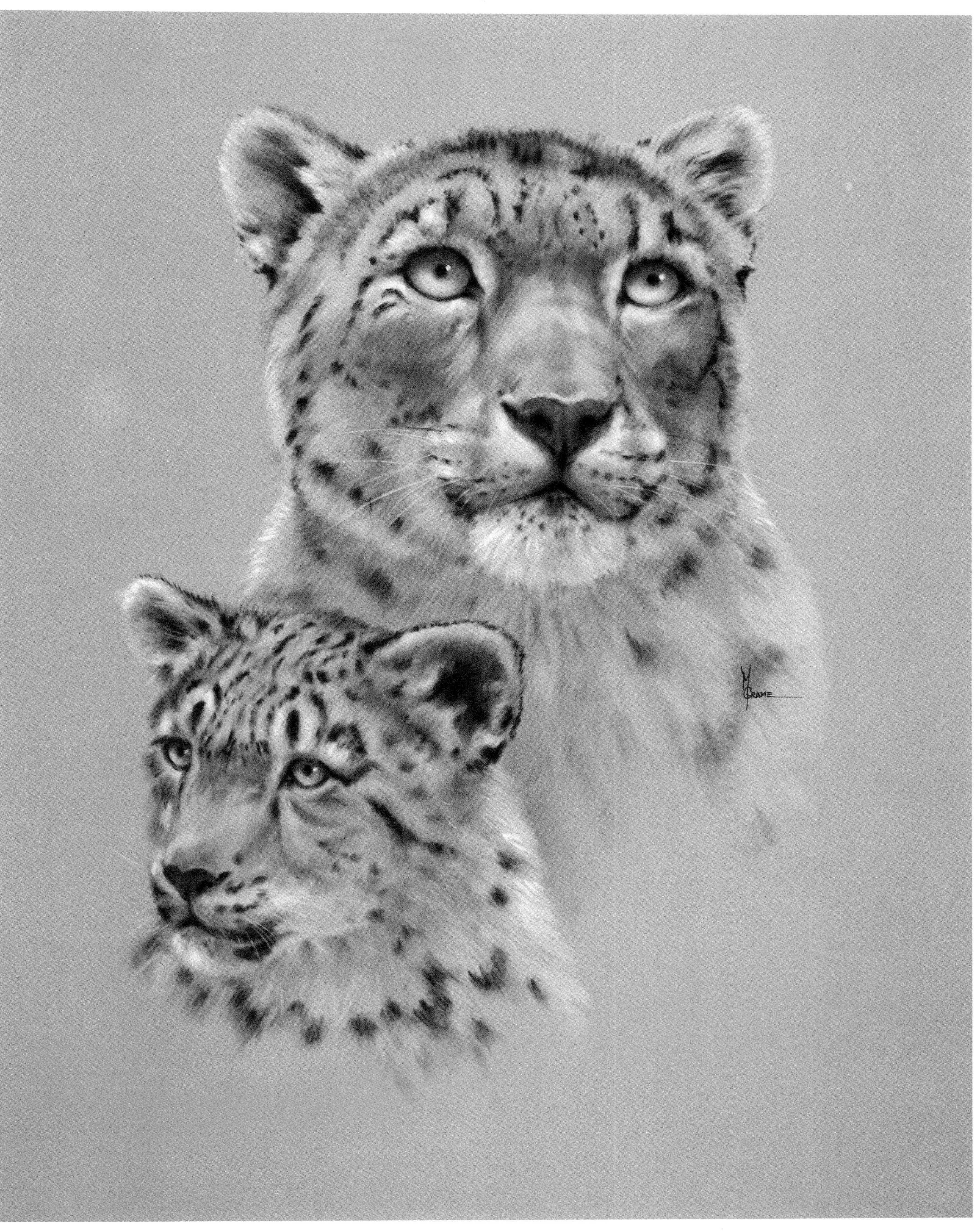

This beautiful green-winged macaw's name is "Chubasco." The colors are magnificent! I chose to do the background (which is worked on white fine-sanded paper) with my airbrush and fast-drying acrylics formulated especially for the airbrush. One way this can be done is to spray the entire area, let it dry, then superimpose the subject on top of it with pastels. Another way (shown at left) is to cover the subject area with frisket film which is peeled off when the paint is dry, leaving the image area clean. An alternative spraying method is to use a mouth atomizer.

At the left is the actual frisket used on this page.

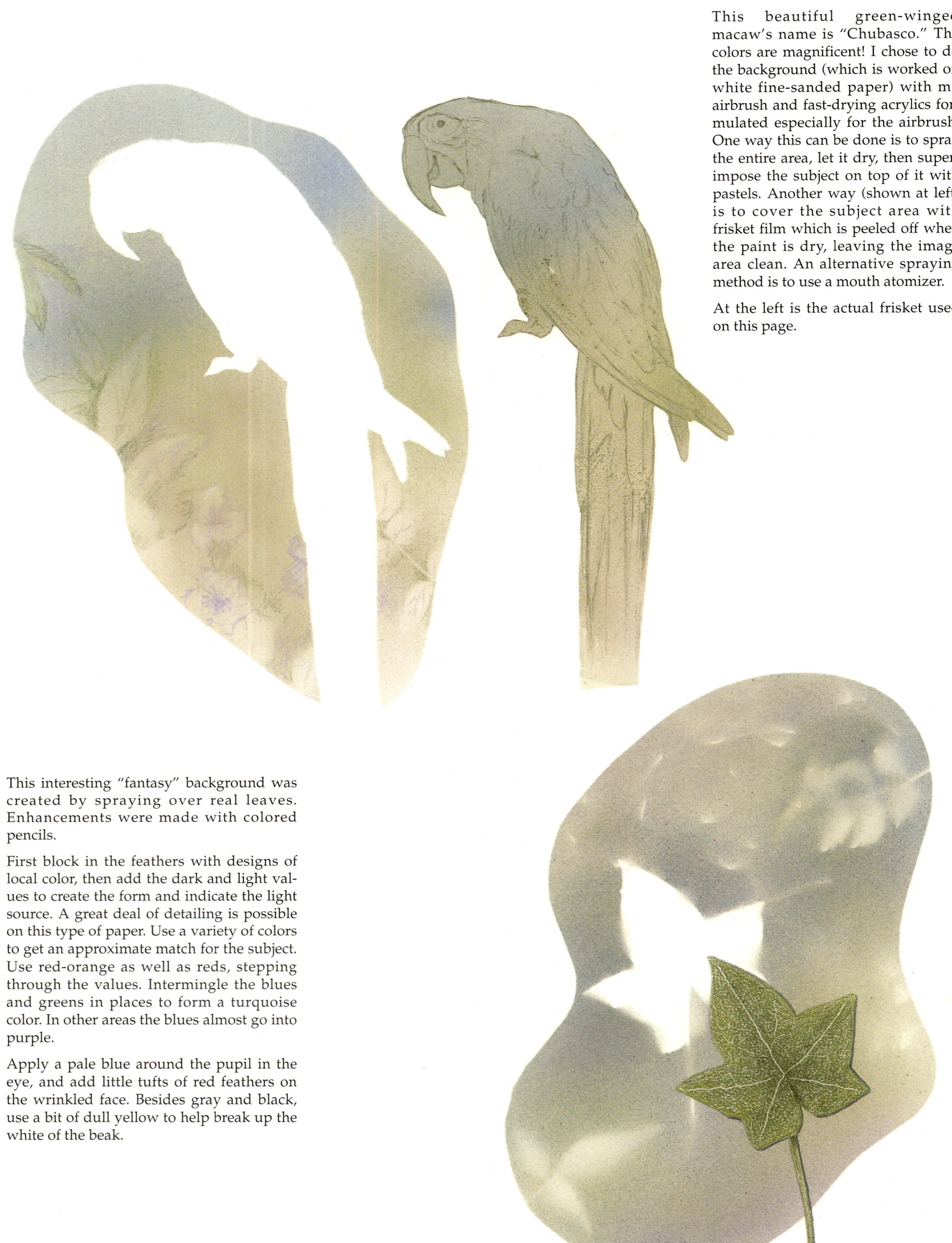

This interesting "fantasy" background was created by spraying over real leaves. Enhancements were made with colored pencils.

First block in the feathers with designs of local color, then add the dark and light values to create the form and indicate the light source. A great deal of detailing is possible on this type of paper. Use a variety of colors to get an approximate match for the subject. Use red-orange as well as reds, stepping through the values. Intermingle the blues and greens in places to form a turquoise color. In other areas the blues almost go into purple.

Apply a pale blue around the pupil in the eye, and add little tufts of red feathers on the wrinkled face. Besides gray and black, use a bit of dull yellow to help break up the white of the beak.

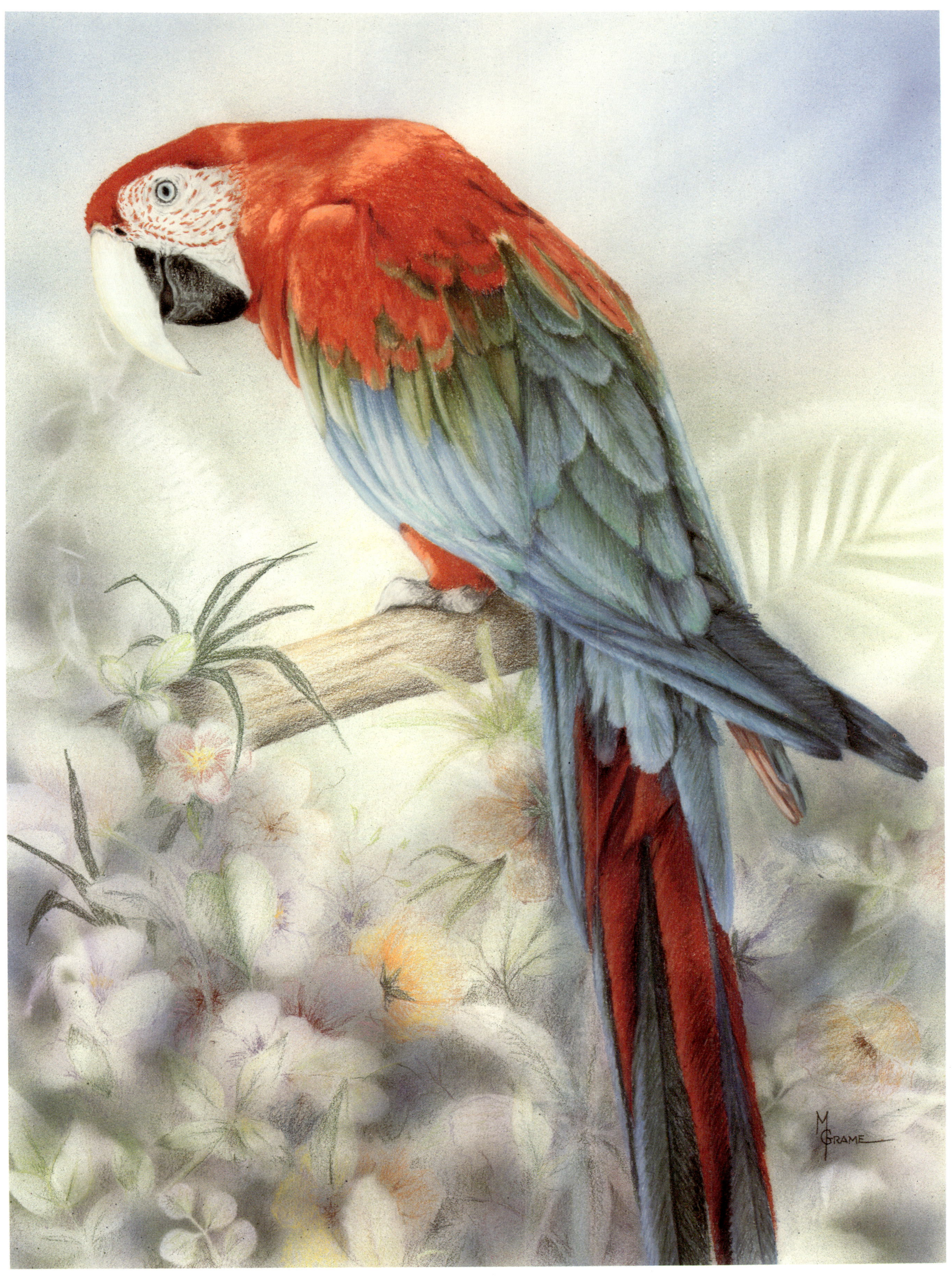
M GRAME

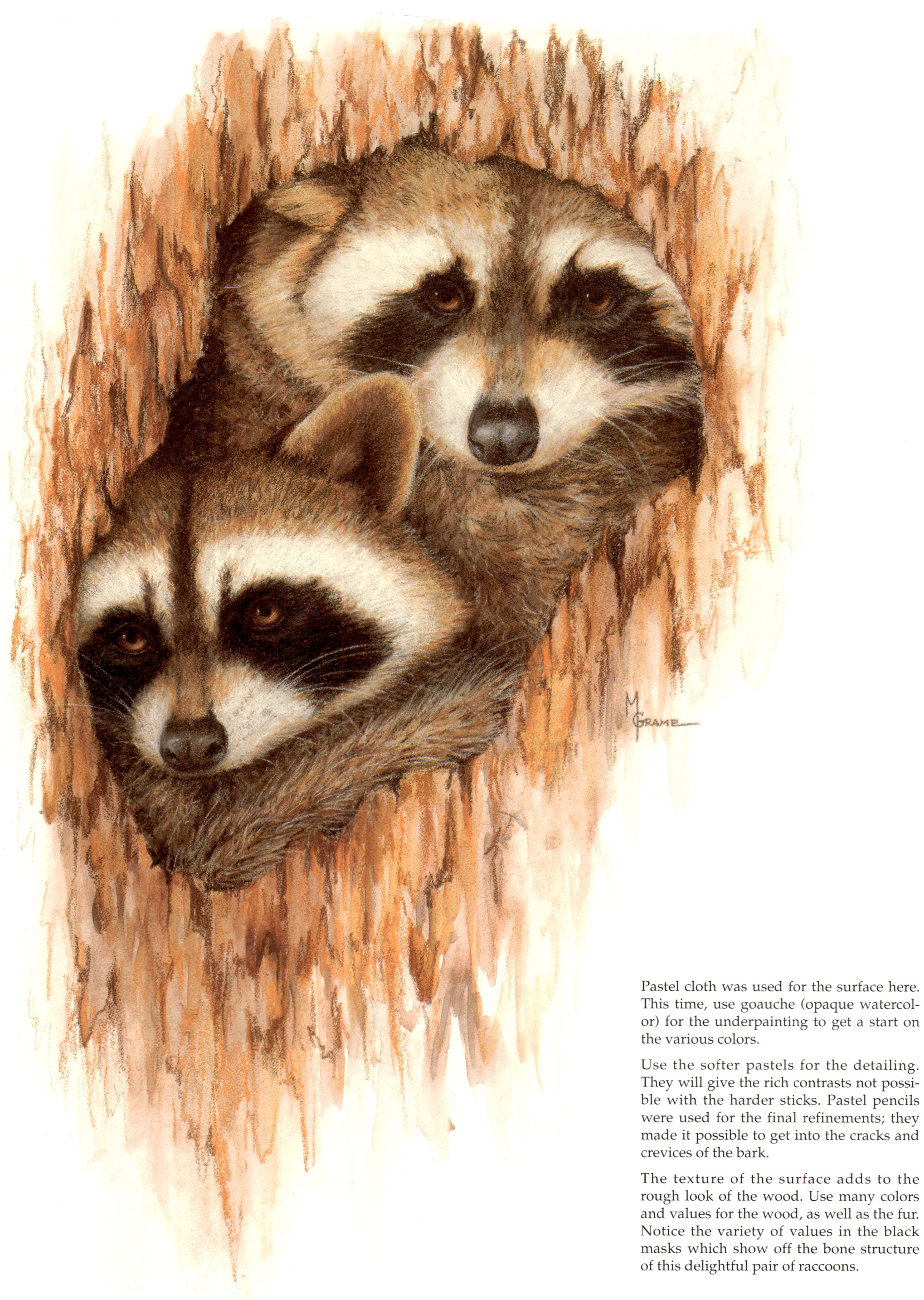

Pastel cloth was used for the surface here. This time, use goauche (opaque watercolor) for the underpainting to get a start on the various colors.

Use the softer pastels for the detailing. They will give the rich contrasts not possible with the harder sticks. Pastel pencils were used for the final refinements; they made it possible to get into the cracks and crevices of the bark.

The texture of the surface adds to the rough look of the wood. Use many colors and values for the wood, as well as the fur. Notice the variety of values in the black masks which show off the bone structure of this delightful pair of raccoons.

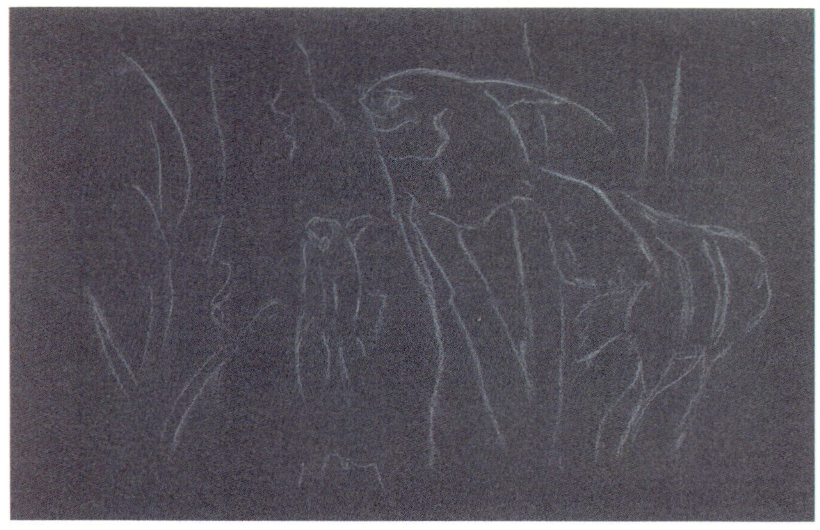

The drawing on this dark colored charcoal-type paper must be light so it will show up.

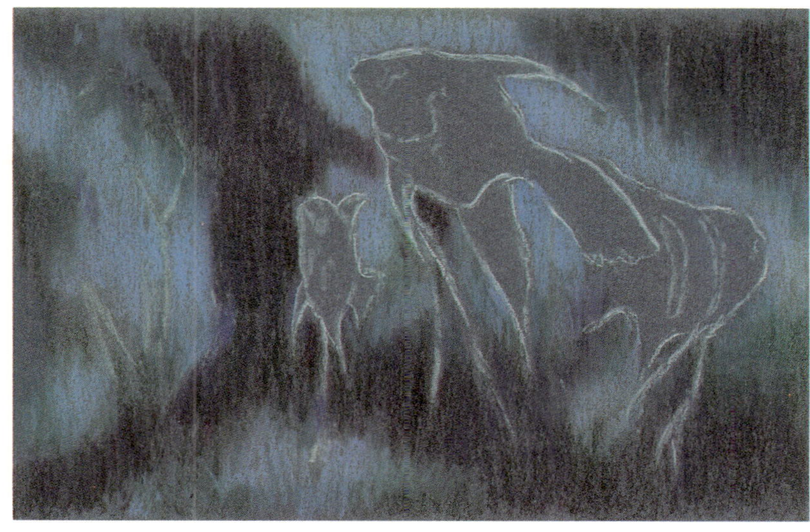

"Scrub" a variety of blues, greens, purples and browns in several values into the background. Do the blending with the pastels themselves to prevent the painting from becoming "muddy."

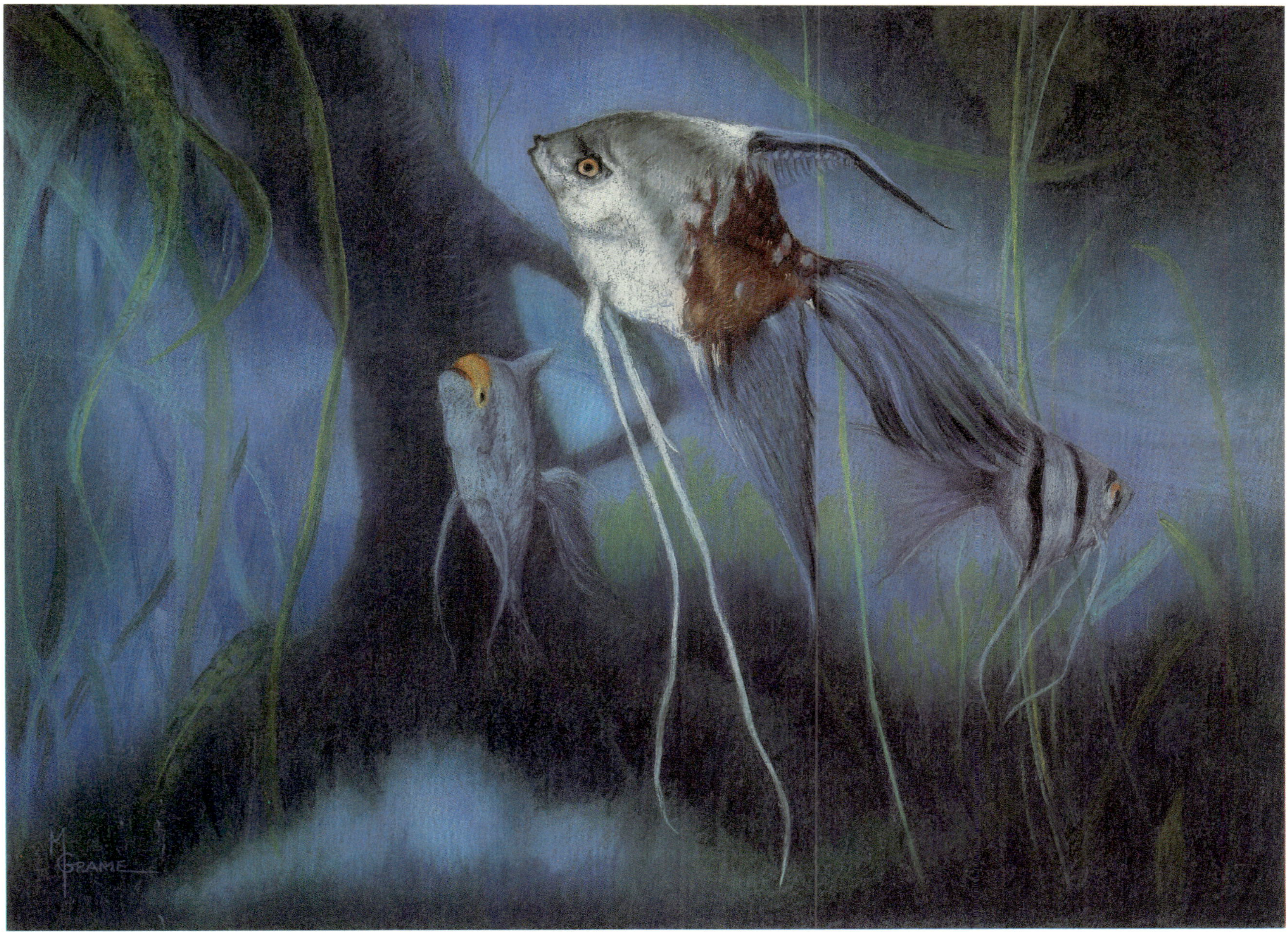

After the background has been softened, add the grasses with greens, blues and yellows, from warm to cool, for as much variety as possible. The fish are defined in great detail. I have kept two of the fish fairly subdued to focus the eye on the main subject. In a completely painted image such as this, pastel pencils can be a great help in bringing certain areas into focus.

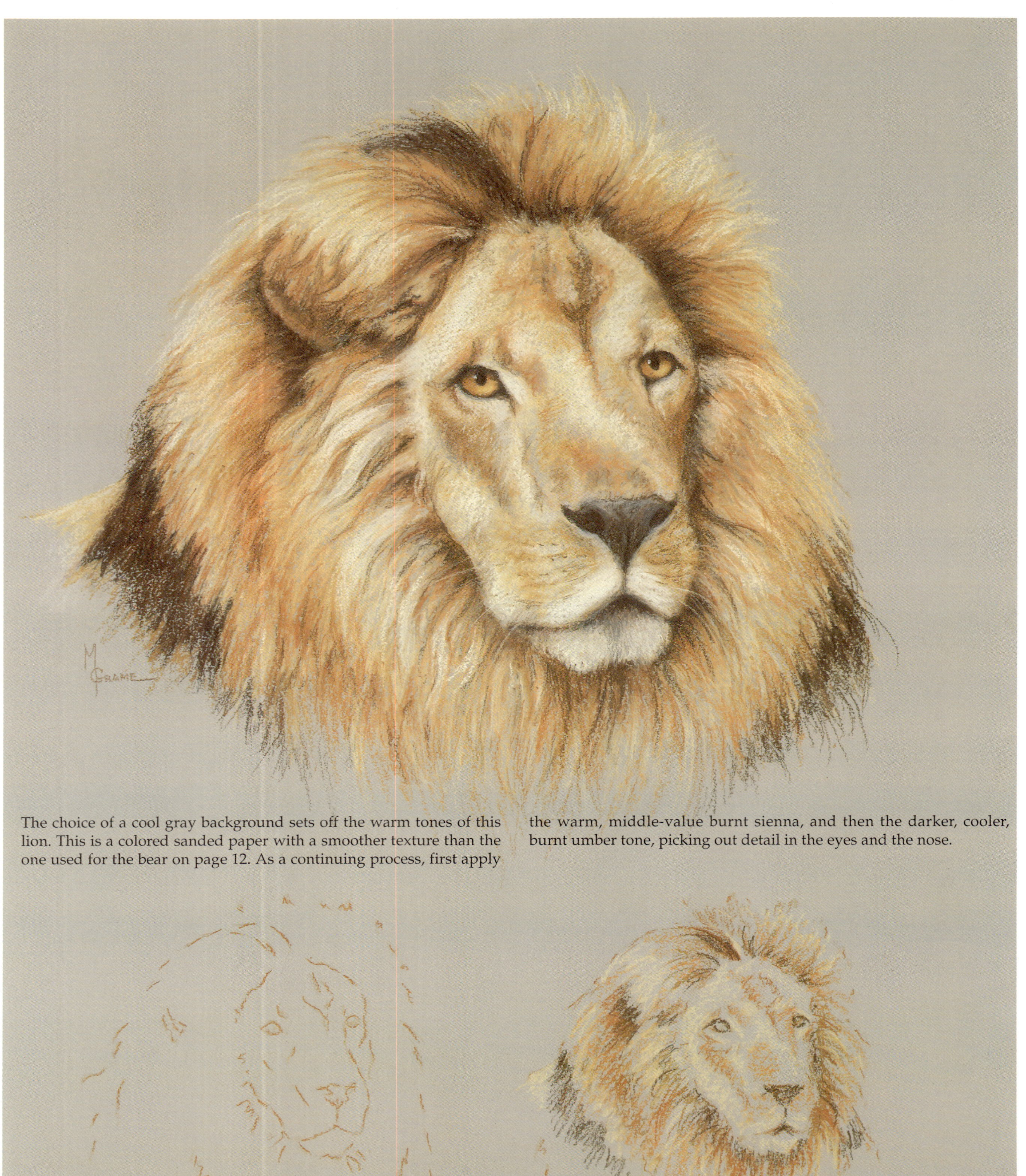

The choice of a cool gray background sets off the warm tones of this lion. This is a colored sanded paper with a smoother texture than the one used for the bear on page 12. As a continuing process, first apply the warm, middle-value burnt sienna, and then the darker, cooler, burnt umber tone, picking out detail in the eyes and the nose.

Transfer the drawing with a warm sienna.

Apply a base-coat of the various colors and values; strive for coverage. Many layers give this a smoother, more complete appearance than the bear on page 12.

It is impossible to duplicate this "one-of-a-kind" background, especially on a small scale, so I will just tell you about it. I started with a piece of green cover stock (heavy charcoal-type paper), then mixed copious amounts of heavily-pigmented watercolor in hooker's green deep, pthalocyanine blue and cerulean blue. I applied the paint with a very large brush, first the green, then "slopping" on the blue. The opaque cerulean went on last, shaking the brush to create the spotting. Margarita salt and light table salt were dropped into the unevenly drying color. The paper really wrinkled, making puddles, but since I was working on my slightly slanted drawing table it didn't run too far, only enough to make some exciting swirls. As the whole thing began to dry (and flattened out), I added splashes of cerulean with Chinese white for the lighter spots. The paint needed to dry COMPLETELY before the salt could be brushed off.

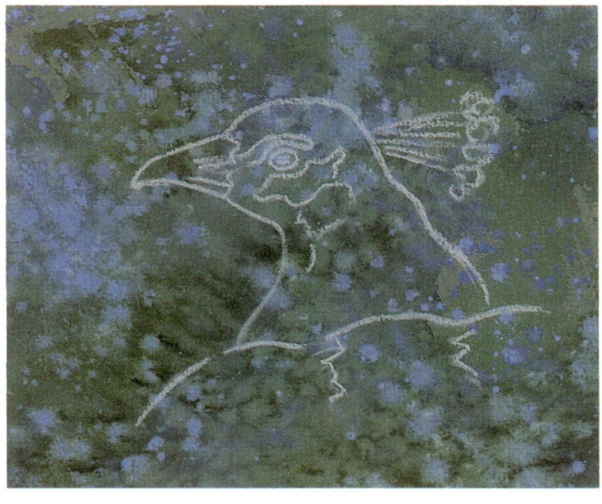

Complete the drawing with a white pastel.

Bring the colors up with pastels, taking advantage of the rough surface of the paper. Apply blues, greens and turquoise on the head and neck. Use black to darken the colors where needed.

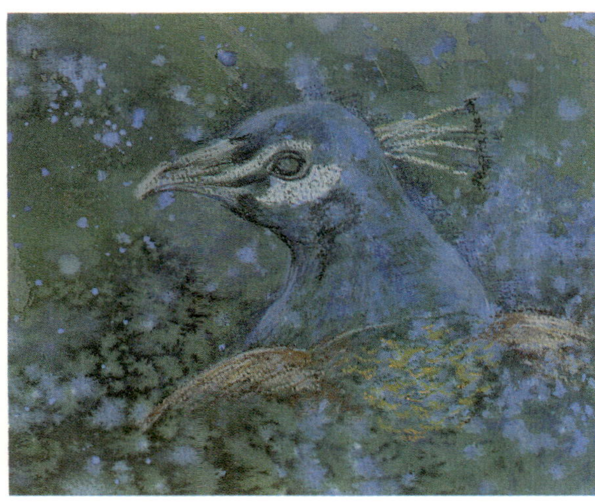

It is fun to develop a subject out of this splashy kind of background. The choice of similar colors here creates a unity in the painting. Strong lights and darks help the definition. Some toning of the background color helped separate the peacock and added aerial perspective.

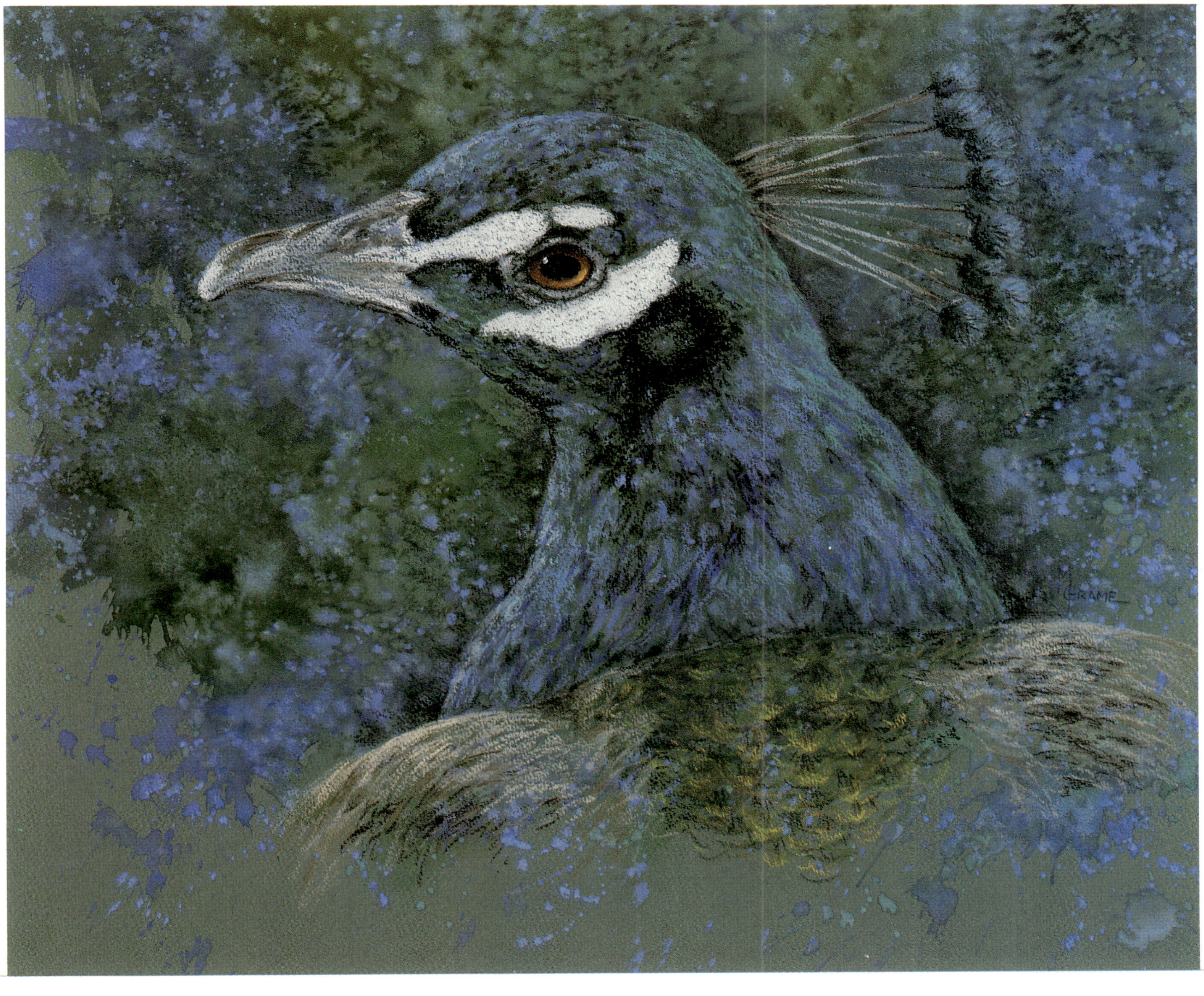

The great horned owl is a lovely creature; the backlighting on this one adds drama to the painting.

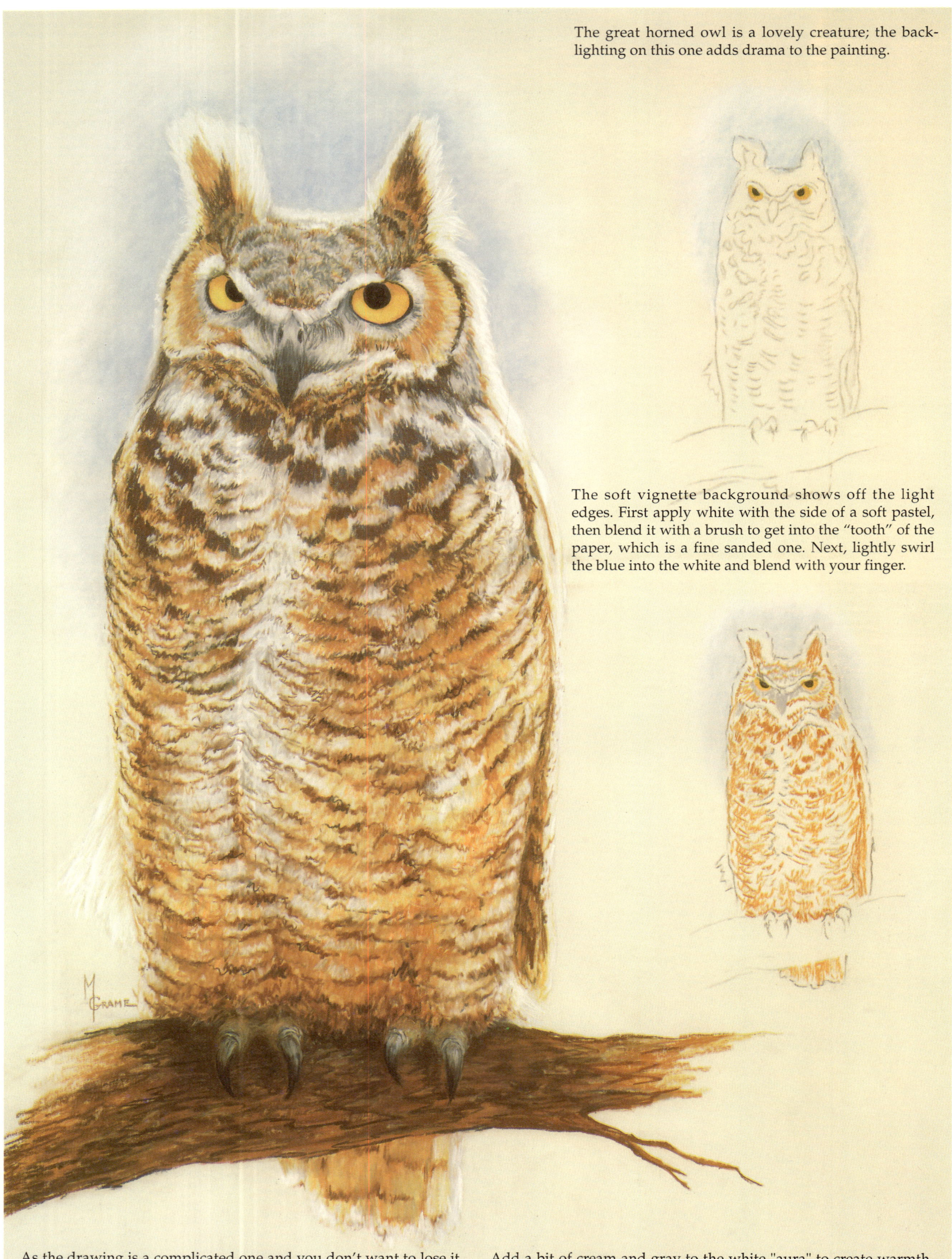

The soft vignette background shows off the light edges. First apply white with the side of a soft pastel, then blend it with a brush to get into the "tooth" of the paper, which is a fine sanded one. Next, lightly swirl the blue into the white and blend with your finger.

As the drawing is a complicated one and you don't want to lose it, begin blocking in the various colors to keep their location. You can get a lot of detail on this kind of paper. Add subtle value tonations, building up the feather design.

Add a bit of cream and gray to the white "aura" to create warmth. The eyes have no highlight because the subject is facing away from the light source, but they glow with an intensity that seems to come from within.

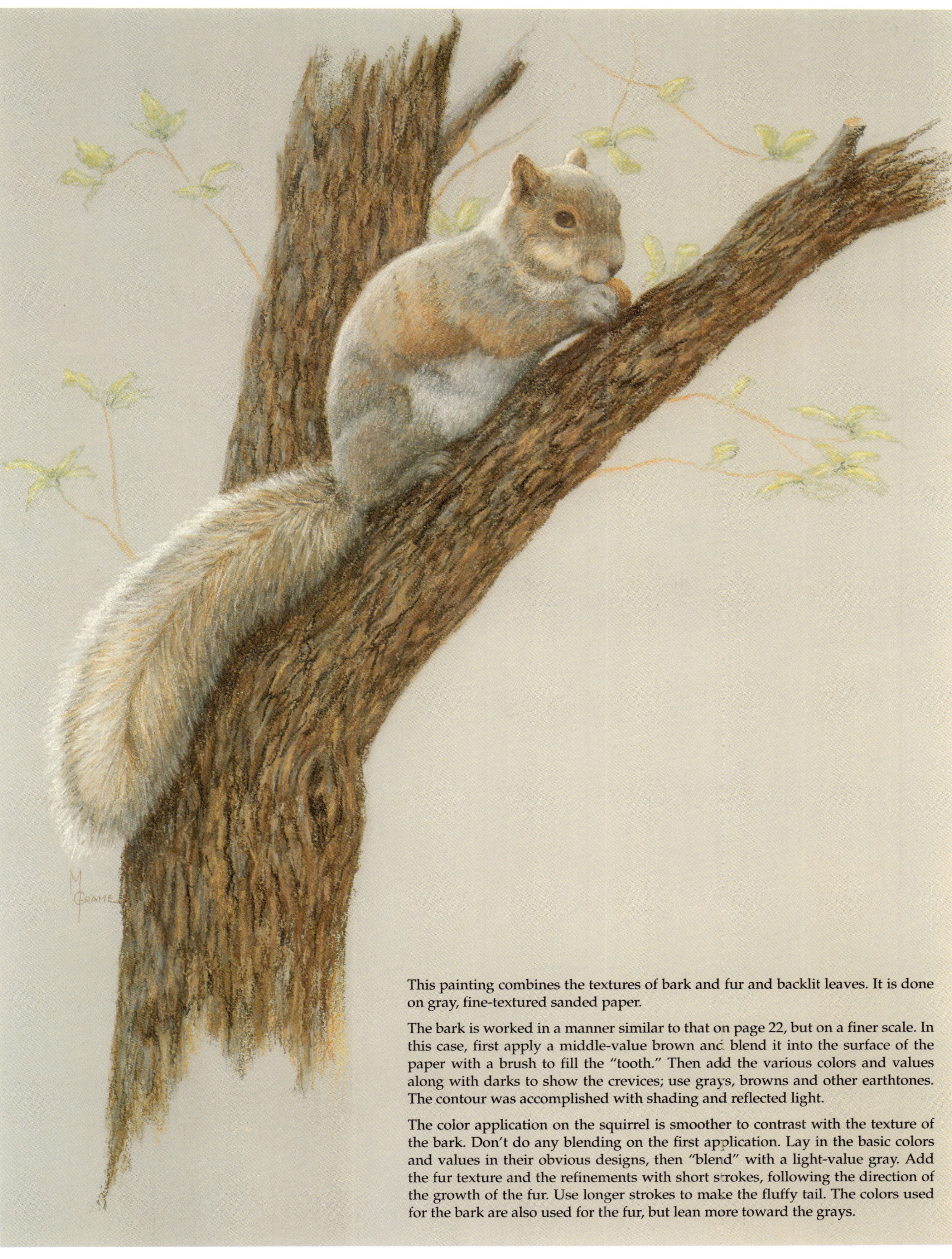

This painting combines the textures of bark and fur and backlit leaves. It is done on gray, fine-textured sanded paper.

The bark is worked in a manner similar to that on page 22, but on a finer scale. In this case, first apply a middle-value brown and blend it into the surface of the paper with a brush to fill the "tooth." Then add the various colors and values along with darks to show the crevices; use grays, browns and other earthtones. The contour was accomplished with shading and reflected light.

The color application on the squirrel is smoother to contrast with the texture of the bark. Don't do any blending on the first application. Lay in the basic colors and values in their obvious designs, then "blend" with a light-value gray. Add the fur texture and the refinements with short strokes, following the direction of the growth of the fur. Use longer strokes to make the fluffy tail. The colors used for the bark are also used for the fur, but lean more toward the grays.

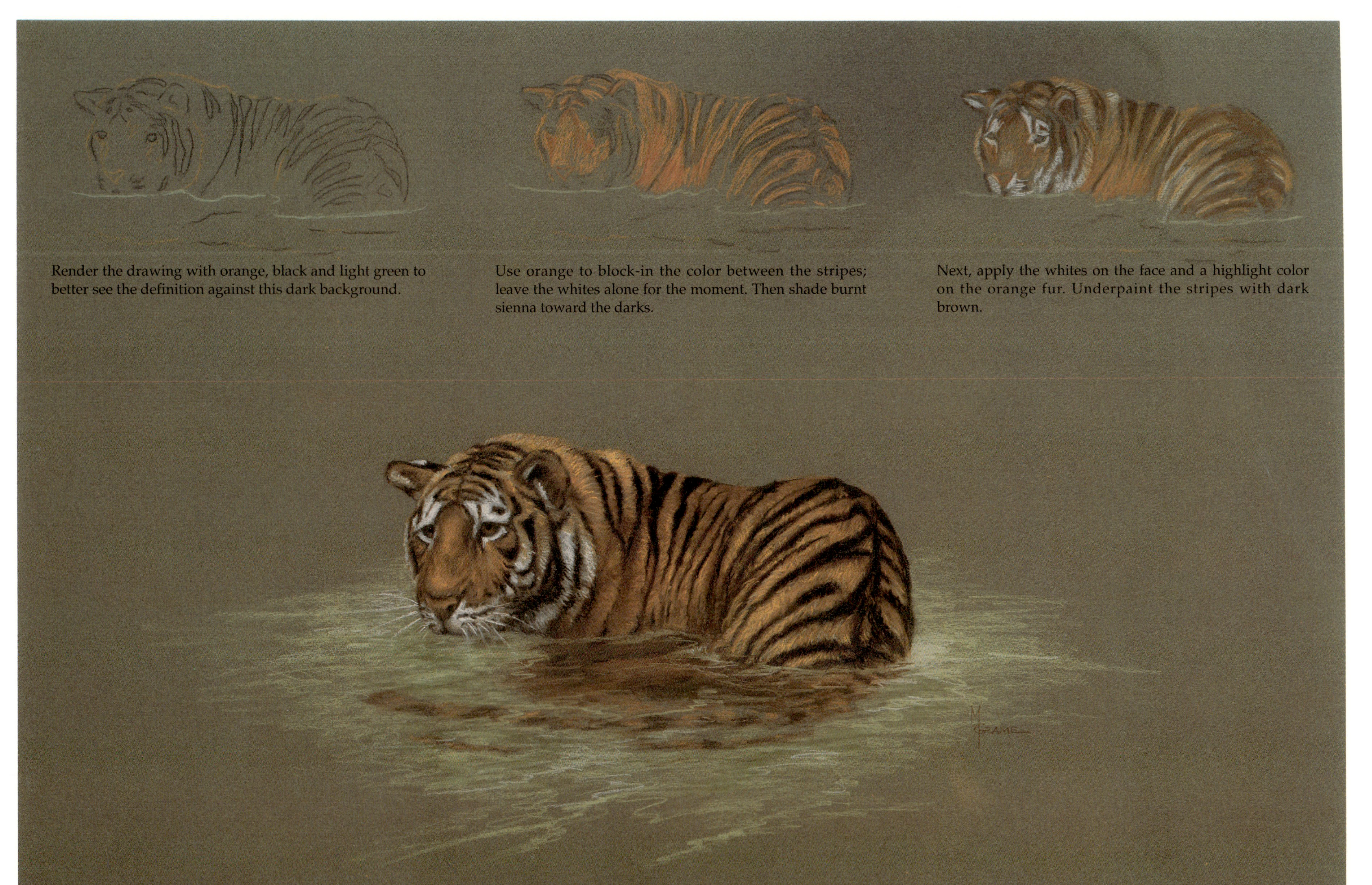

Render the drawing with orange, black and light green to better see the definition against this dark background.

Use orange to block-in the color between the stripes; leave the whites alone for the moment. Then shade burnt sienna toward the darks.

Next, apply the whites on the face and a highlight color on the orange fur. Underpaint the stripes with dark brown.

The fascinating part of this tiger picture is the broken image of the body and the tail underwater. The greenish water is a beautiful contrast to the warm tones of the subject and is supported by the gray-green charcoal paper used here.

Apply black over the brown-based stripes, then use pastel pencils to make refinements to the eyes, the nose and the whiskers. Gray some of the whites to show off the light source. "Feather" the colors, one over the other, in the direction of the fur growth. Repeat the tiger colors in the water to form the patterns of the underwater tail and legs. Use a variety of greens in the water.

BACK

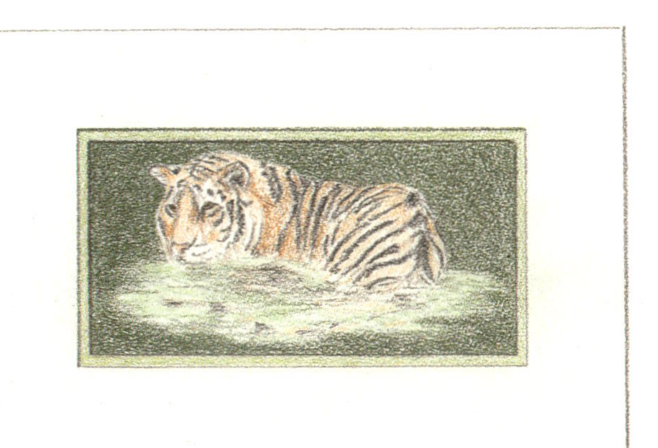

FRONT

Framing Pastels

Pastels should be protected behind glass and separated from the glass with either mats or spacers. The "air space" will prevent damage to the painting should it "sweat" inside the glass. I Seal the back of the frame with paper if it is a wooden frame; however, I often frame my artwork with modular metal frames.

Some surfaces have a rigid backing which can be an added advantage in framing. If your work is on paper, treat it as you would a watercolor. Suspend the paper from "hinges" of linen tape attached on the back at the top of the mat. Taping all the way around can cause buckling with atmospheric changes; if it is suspended, it can expand and contract.

The Spray Controversy

To spray or not to spray? There are opposing views on this subject. Many artists feel spraying weakens the lights and increases the darks. Some types of sprays will do this. You will need to experiment with various brands of sprays. A regular charcoal fixative is not recommended—look for a specialty spray, paying attention to the suggested uses on the can. Some painters who do not spray layer the pigment and pound on the back of the surface to get rid of the excess pigment. Some artists spray several times as the painting progresses, while others spray only the finished product.

Spraying Problems

When spraying, it is best to lay the painting flat on the ground, then from a standing position, fog on the spray, keeping the can in motion. Apply several light layers, allowing each to dry before applying the next. Always spray a mist off to the side before spraying your painting to make sure the spray is even and fine and is not "spattering." This can leave dots all over your painting, which is heartbreaking. Be sure to use the spray in a well-ventilated area and wear a mask, if possible. It is very dangerous to breathe the vapors. You may want to spray if you enter competitions where the paintings will be handled by many different people—some of whom, unfortunately, do not know how to handle this delicate medium. Even so, I have had paintings returned "powdered off" against the glass and all over the mats.

Storage

You can store unframed pastels in an appropriate size tie portfolio, separated with tracing paper (vellum) or similar non-yellowing paper. As the pictures will be "sandwiched" when tied, they will not slip against each other and smear.

If you are lucky enough to have an empty closet, an alternative storage method might be to hang the paintings from wire coat hangers with clothespins.

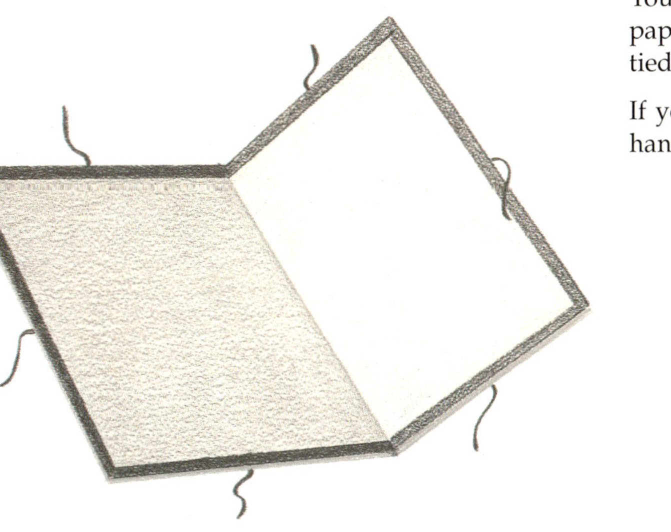

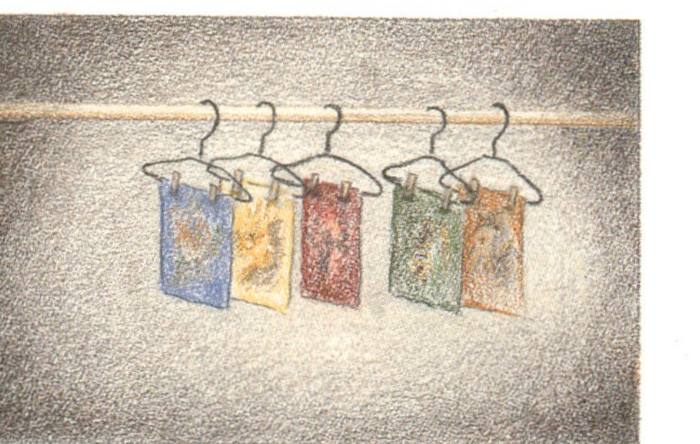

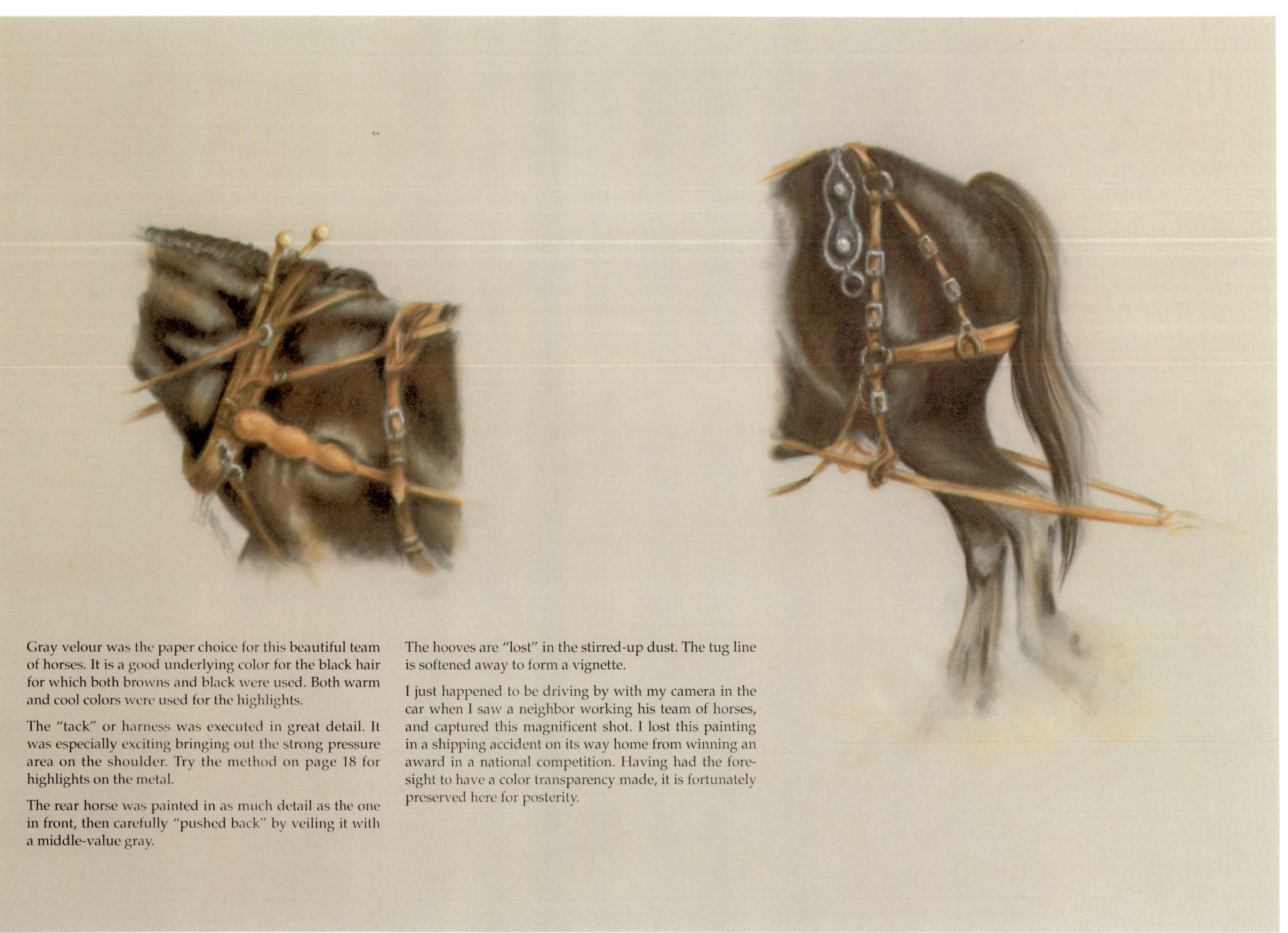

Gray velour was the paper choice for this beautiful team of horses. It is a good underlying color for the black hair for which both browns and black were used. Both warm and cool colors were used for the highlights.

The "tack" or harness was executed in great detail. It was especially exciting bringing out the strong pressure area on the shoulder. Try the method on page 18 for highlights on the metal.

The rear horse was painted in as much detail as the one in front, then carefully "pushed back" by veiling it with a middle-value gray.

The hooves are "lost" in the stirred-up dust. The tug line is softened away to form a vignette.

I just happened to be driving by with my camera in the car when I saw a neighbor working his team of horses, and captured this magnificent shot. I lost this painting in a shipping accident on its way home from winning an award in a national competition. Having had the foresight to have a color transparency made, it is fortunately preserved here for posterity.

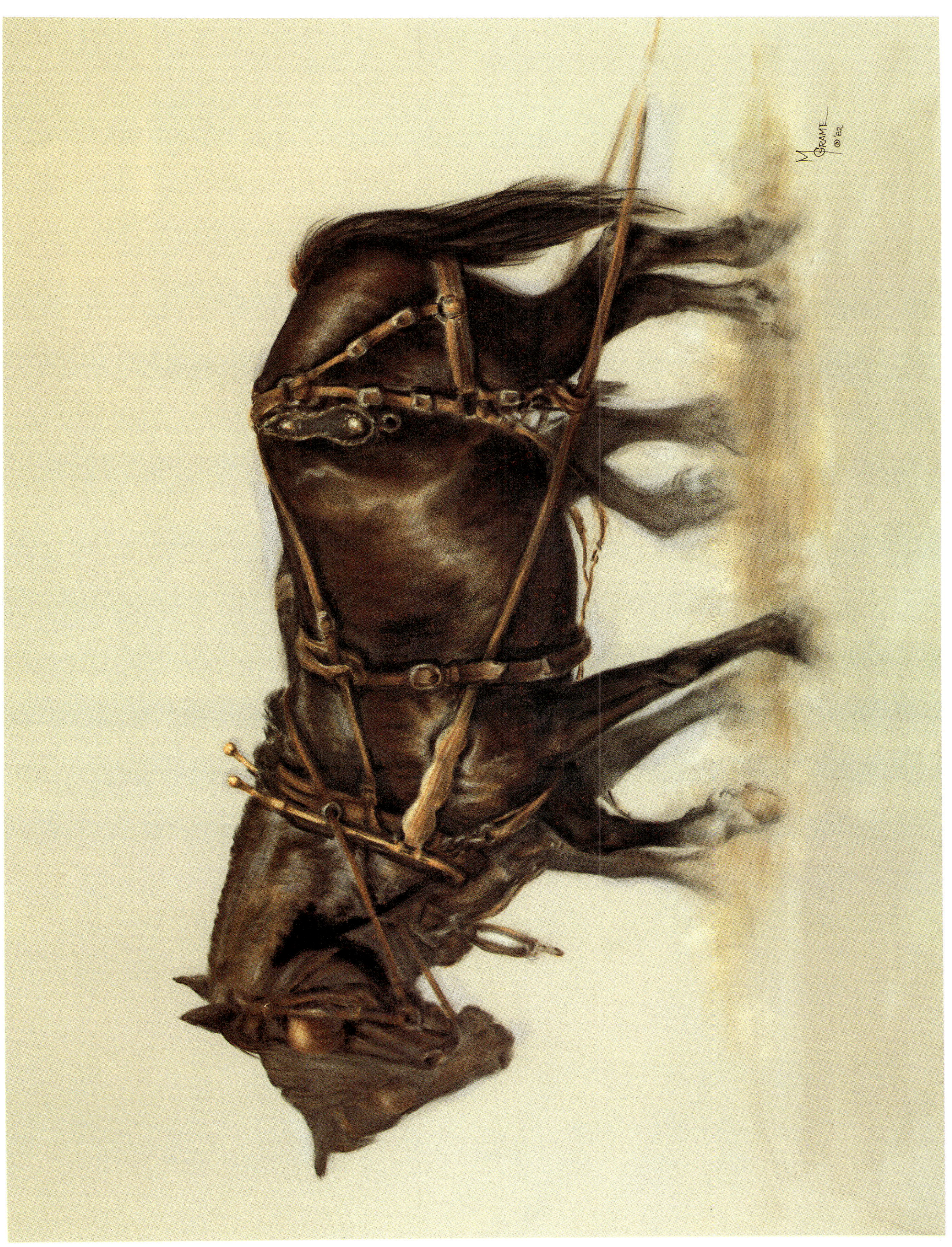
M GRAME
©'82

More Ways To Learn With

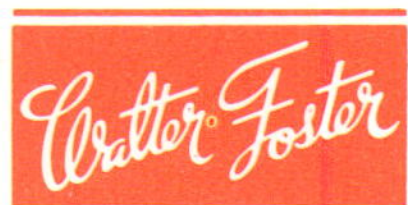

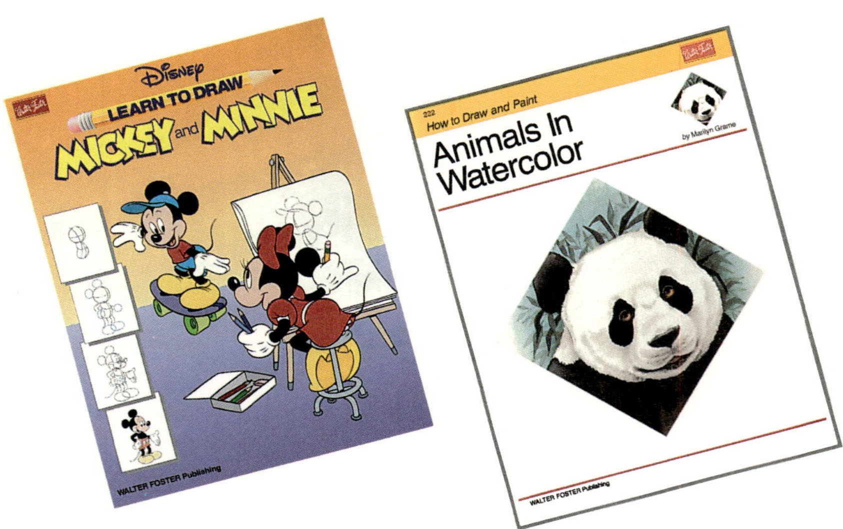

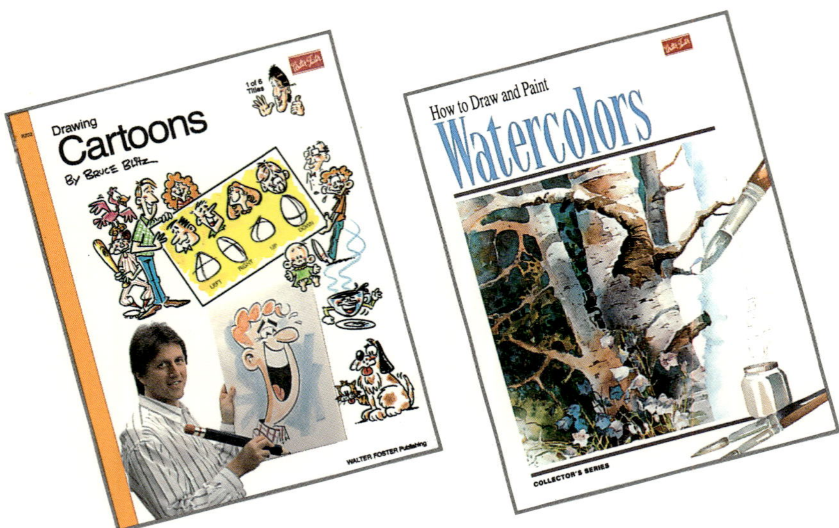

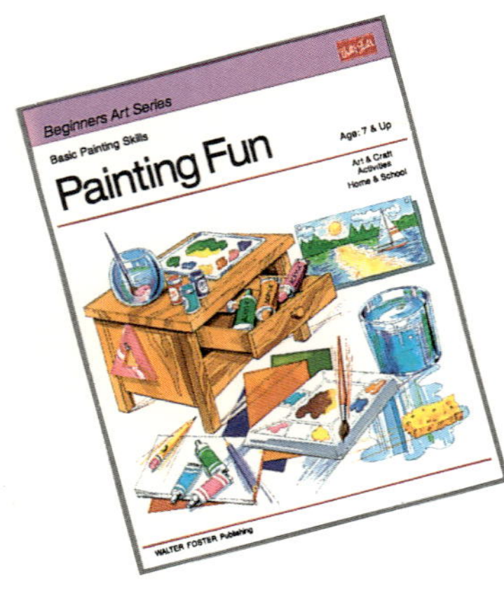

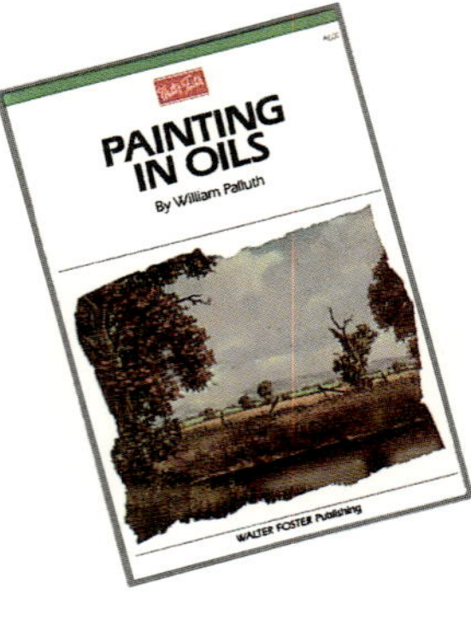

WALTER FOSTER Publishing...
The most recognized name in art publishing for more than 74 years!

Disney Learn To Draw Series

The Walt Disney Company© and Walter Foster Publishing have combined their talents to create this wonderful new series of art books for children.

Each book in the **Disney Learn To Draw Series** features a different set of characters and includes step-by-step instructions and illustrations, fun ways to use action lines, tips on outlining and coloring, and hints on how to create different poses and expressions.

Children will be entertained for hours as they practice drawing their favorite Disney characters—and they'll love showing off their very own "masterpieces"!

Paperback, 32 pages, 10-1/4" x 13-3/4"

How To Series

No matter what the medium or the subject matter, we have a book in our **"How To" Series** to fit every artist's needs.

Filled with step-by-step illustrations of techniques for various media, these books address the full art spectrum—pen and ink, pencil, pastel, charcoal, watercolor, acrylic and oil—and they address all skill levels. Their easy-to-follow instructional style takes the beginning artist through the fundamentals of outlining, shading, form and perspective. And, as each lesson builds on the newly developed skill of the preceding lesson, the books move into the more sophisticated rendering techniques sought by the advanced artist.

Paperback, 32 pages, 10-1/4" x 13-3/4"

Blitz Cartoon Series

This new series is designed for people who just can't stop doodling! Bruce Blitz, creator and host of the Emmy-nominated Public Television series, "*Blitz On Cartooning*," believes that anyone with desire and a positive attitude can learn to draw—so he has developed these four new books demonstrating fun and easy methods for turning "doodles" into finished drawings, cartoons and comic strips.

The **Blitz Cartoon Series** is perfect for people of all ages who like to draw, but believe they "can't even draw a straight line."

Paperback, 48 pages, 10-1/4" x 13-3/4"

Collector's Series

Each book in the **Collector's Series** contains a selection of some of the most popular books from our "How To" Series—all combined in a high quality, hardcover edition.

Compiled from many of our bestsellers, each of these books begins with the fundamentals of the particular medium—pencil, watercolor, oil, or animation—then explores the techniques, styles and subjects of the various artists.

The **Collector's Series** was inspired by, and designed for, the serious art enthusiast.

Hardcover, 144 pages, 10-1/4" x 13-3/4"

Beginners Art Series

The **Beginners Art Series** is a great way to introduce children to the wonderful world of art. Designed for ages 6 and up, this popular series helps children develop strong tactile and visual skills while they have a lot of fun! Each book explores a different medium and features exciting projects with simple step-by-step instructions and illustrations.

Paperback, 64 pages, 8-3/8" x 10-7/8"

Artist's Library Series

Serious instruction for serious artists—that's what the **Artist's Library Series** is all about! The books in this series can help both beginning and advanced artists expand their creativity, conquer technical obstacles, and investigate new media. Each book explores the materials and methods of a specific medium and includes step-by-step demonstrations, helpful tips, and comprehensive instructions.

The books of the **Artist's Library Series** are helpful additions to any artist's reference library.

Paperback, 64 pages, 6-1/2" x 9-1/2"

©The Walt Disney Company